Can't ... More Money?

CAN'T WE JUST PRINT MORE MONEY?

Economics in Ten Simple Questions

Rupal Patel and Jack Meaning
The Bank of England

Cornerstone Press

1 3 5 7 9 10 8 6 4 2

Cornerstone Press
20 Vauxhall Bridge Road
London SW1V 2SA

Cornerstone Press is part of the Penguin Random House
group of companies whose addresses can be found at
global.penguinrandomhouse.com.

Penguin
Random House
UK

First published by Cornerstone Press in 2022

www.penguin.co.uk

A CIP catalogue record for this book is available from
the British Library.

ISBN 9781847943385

Illustrations by Adam Doughty

Typeset in 10.5/16.5 pt Casus Pro
by Integra Software Services Pvt. Ltd, Pondicherry

Printed and bound in Great Britain by Clays Ltd, Elcograf S.p.A.

The authorised representative in the EEA is Penguin Random House
Ireland, Morrison Chambers, 32 Nassau Street, Dublin D02 YH68.

Penguin Random House is committed to a sustainable future for
our business, our readers and our planet. This book is made from
Forest Stewardship Council® certified paper.

To our families, for their unending support and encouragement. And to all aspiring economists hoping to understand and shape the world around them.

Contents

Foreword by the Governor of the Bank of England

My secondary school education took place in the 1970s, which was not a good time for economies around the world. I remember doing my homework by candlelight during the three-day week, and experiencing the effects of inflation hitting more than 20 per cent. It left a lasting impression, making me acutely aware of the impact of economics on people's lives.

You won't be surprised to know, then, that I'm a great advocate of economic literacy. Even a relatively basic understanding of economics can be useful. On one level, economics can help you to make a bit more sense of the news – whether it's decoding acronyms like GDP and QE, or helping to explain why the economy is growing or shrinking. More broadly, economics can give you tools to help you make better decisions, whether about money or pretty much anything else. If you want to dig deeper, economics can also be a fascinating and enjoyable discipline about which to learn (but then I would say that . . .).

Which brings me to this book; something of a first for the Bank of England. It looks quite different from most things the Bank has published over the last three centuries. For a start, there's only one equation in its 320 pages, and that's a pretty straightforward formula containing just as many letters as a Wordle. But this book hasn't come out of the blue. Rather, it's part of a wider effort to help explain our work – and the workings of the economy more broadly – in a way that more people can easily understand.

For example, we now produce versions of our flagship reports, such as our quarterly summary of how the UK economy is performing, in a shorter, more accessible format, using everyday language and simple graphics and illustrations. We've also created a 'Knowledge Bank' section on our website, which provides an introduction to money, banks, inflation and interest rates, among other things. It has proved popular, attracting more page views than almost any other part of our website. If you enjoy this book, I'd urge you to take a look.

Alas, not everyone regularly checks the Bank of England website, or eagerly awaits publication of our quarterly economic reports, so we've been making an effort to reach people in other ways. The Bank's Deputy Governors and I regularly participate in our Citizens' Panels across the country, which are open to any member of the public to attend. We hold these so that we can hear first-hand from people about their experiences of all aspects of the economy, from the cost of living to how easy it is to find a job. They also allow us to explain the decisions we have taken, and for people to ask us anything they like about our work. Alongside these events we also run Community Forums in partnership with charities across the UK, which help us to understand how the people they support are being impacted by the economy.

This book is the latest of the Bank's attempts to spread the word about economics. Over the past few years, we have developed an extensive education programme that introduces young people to the basics of money management and key economic concepts. We also have more than 500 Bank colleagues who deliver talks in state schools around the UK, discussing a range of topics including the work of the Bank and their own career journeys. In this book, we've drawn on our experiences creating the education programme to produce an accessible, one-stop guide to basic economics.

I try to do these school talks myself regularly, and the next time I do I'll be carrying a copy of this book with me. Hopefully, some of the students will have seen it before: we plan to send one to every state school in the country. And, if they have, I hope they'll have discovered how economics is a subject that can help us both to understand the world around us and to tackle some of the biggest challenges facing it, from poverty to climate change. Who knows, it might even encourage one or two to think about studying it in greater detail. One day they could end up working alongside Rupal, Jack and me here at the Bank of England.

I've long felt that working at the Bank provides a unique opportunity to use economics to 'promote the good of the people of the United Kingdom', as our rather grand mission statement puts it. It is because of our unique role, and the responsibility that comes with it, that I am so delighted that the Bank has produced this book. We're indebted to Rupal and Jack, and the dozens of colleagues who have worked with them on this project, for producing a fun and informative introduction to a discipline that – although often ridiculed, especially when things don't pan out as expected – I'm convinced helps make the world a better place. After reading it, I hope you'll understand why.

Andrew Bailey
Governor of the Bank of England

Introduction
Economics, everywhere

The Bank of England looks like a forbidding place. Located in Threadneedle Street at the heart of the City of London, the Bank's building is adorned with classical columns, intricately carved stonework and ornate statues. Its grand front entrance gives it the feel of a fortress; its huge bronze doors, usually flanked by security guards, seem designed to deter passers-by from entering.

For over three centuries, the Bank has stood on this site as a symbol of the English – and later British – economic establishment. Yet for all that, the Bank of England's headquarters is an office like any other. Every weekday morning, hundreds of slightly nerdy economists and their colleagues pass through its imposing doors. And at lunchtime every day, these Bank staffers, just like all other office workers up and down the country, file back out to stretch their legs, escape their screens and search for something to eat.

I

If you were to follow one of those hungry economists on their lunch break, you would discover that economics doesn't just matter within the walls of the Bank of England. It is everywhere. Let's start with what to eat. Within the Square Mile of the City of London there are over 500 cafes, restaurants and takeaway venues, serving an incredible variety of food from Japanese sushi to Italian antipasti, Middle Eastern mezze to good old British fish and chips.[1] But who decides what is going to be on offer? How do the various shop owners know whether it is better to sell doughnuts or cupcakes? And why are there a dozen coffee shops on each street, but only one place selling jellied eels?

The answer starts with decisions – all the individual decisions made by the thousands of people looking for their lunches. Our hungry economist decides to opt for a meal deal and heads for the closest supermarket rather than one of the trendier, more expensive artisanal bakeries nearby. This may seem like a mundane choice but behind it is an economic decision about how to best spend your time and money, given a set of personal preferences and a budget constraint.

While queuing to pay for their sandwich and crisps (the first rule of economics is that there is no such thing as a free lunch), our economist takes a second to think about how their meal deal made its way to the supermarket's shelves. Someone had to grow the wheat to make the bread. Then it had to be transported to a factory, where workers baked the raw grain. The bread was then combined with other ingredients, many sourced from overseas, into a sandwich – before being popped in a box perhaps made in a completely different factory and transported to the supermarket.

In other words, hundreds – perhaps thousands – of individual acts and interactions have gone into creating our economist's sandwich, and it is unlikely that any of the people or companies involved had done it through a desire to make sure our economist have a tasty lunch. This is the power of what economists call markets. They have a way of coordinating millions of individual decisions to get an outcome that, in theory at least, suits everyone. The result: a sandwich that's delivered to the supermarket at precisely the moment it is desired.

Leaving the supermarket, our economist sets out to find somewhere pleasant to eat. Maybe they should sit by the river? They walk south towards the Thames and plonk themselves on a bench to watch the water rush past. The river looks particularly high today, perhaps it's high tide. But our economist also knows that in general the Thames is higher now than ever before. Since the Bank of England was established in 1694, the high-water level of the river has risen by more than 1.5m.[2] Rising sea levels globally mean that this pattern is only likely to continue.

This is the flipside of those very forces that allowed our economist to get their sandwich. On this occasion, the cumulative decisions of billions of humans haven't led to a positive outcome (food delivered on time) but instead to a negative one (climate change). Economics can help us understand the forces that led to this happening, as well as how we should respond.

Having finished their meal deal, our economist decides to go for a stroll along the river. They walk east, pressing on past the Tower of London and Tower Bridge until they find themselves entering London's Docklands. Just a few decades previously, these docks would have been a hive of activity; filled with thousands of workers lifting goods in and out of ships, and forklifting crates from place to place. For much of the twentieth century, such industrial hubs were one of the engines of economic growth, leading to an inexorable increase in the amount of stuff that the British economy was producing. The way that the dockworkers' labour, the technology they used and the docks themselves combined to increase the size of the economy is one of the great themes of economics.

Along with docks in cities like Liverpool, Belfast and Cardiff, these docks made Britain the commercial powerhouse of the world. They would have sent steel and coal, cars and mechanical parts to cities around the globe – ranging from Calcutta to Canberra. However, today the docks are much quieter than they used to be, and most of the warehouses have been converted into trendy restaurants and offices. Why did Britain used to send so many goods around the world? And why do we send out relatively fewer manufactured goods today, while importing most of our T-shirts and fruit from overseas? The economics of trade – and the principle of 'comparative advantage' – can help to explain this conundrum.

It's nearly time to get back to work, but before beginning the walk back to the office, our economist decides they need a caffeine hit. They stop at a kiosk to buy a coffee, but they have no need to rummage for coins in their pockets to pay, they simply tap their phone. Our economist takes a second to marvel at the fact that someone is willing to give up a physical item – one that has taken time and effort to produce – in exchange for a Jedi-esque swipe of a mobile. How does this digital wizardry relate to the coins and notes of old, or even the bars of gold that sit in the vaults of the Bank of England? The nature of money is one of the biggest economic questions hiding in plain sight in our everyday lives.

Before turning around for the walk back to their desk, our economist looks east along the river. On the horizon are the skyscrapers of Canary Wharf, in East London, emblazoned with the names of some of the world's biggest banks. These names will be recognisable to almost every-one with a bank account – and even those without one. They appear on high streets up and down the country. They are the institutions we trust to look after our hard-earned money and savings. They are the same names that we go to when we need to take out a mortgage, or borrow for our businesses. They also create the vast majority of the money that we use in our daily lives – something that most people who handle that money don't even realise.

As they wander back to the office, our economist's mind turns to the afternoon ahead. The Bank of England's panel of decision-makers is going to decide today if they want to change the rate of interest. This decision will have con-sequences for every single person that our economist passed on their lunchtime walk. It could change how much interest they are earning on their savings, the cost of their mortgage, even the exchange rate they will encounter the next time they go on holiday. And yet many people have no idea how this decision is made, or the wide array of ways in which it will affect them.

Just before they step back into the Bank, our economist bumps into a friend from school – it turns out she works around the corner. They haven't seen each other in years. They discuss the weather, their social plans and the economist's job in the Bank. Before parting ways, the friend asks our economist one final question: 'I've never understood why you can't just print more money?' Our economist decides they don't have time to get into that now, they have a meeting to get to. Maybe someone should write a book that explains the answer.

Our economist's friend could be forgiven for not knowing why we can't just endlessly print money. Economics affects all of us every day of our lives. Each time you make a choice about whether or not to work, whether to spend some money today or save it for tomorrow, go out for a meal or cook one at home, you are making an economic decision. Big economic forces, like global trade, taxation and government spending, are influencing almost every aspect of your life. Yet all too many of us don't know what economics actually *is*.

A narrow definition of economics is that it is the study of scarcity. It is how we work out how best to allocate the finite things that we have around us – whether that's land, or people, or time. A broader definition is that it is everything: the cumulative effect of all of the billions of decisions that humans make every day, and the way they interact with everything else in the world. The truth, as ever, is somewhere in the middle. At least as far back as the ancient Greeks, humans have been trying to make sense of the world around them through the lens of organising stuff.

In fact, the word economics comes from the Greek – literally, 'household management' comes from '*eco*', meaning home; and from '*nomos*', meaning accounts. This focus on organising stuff and the connection to people's everyday lives is at the heart of economics: it is how we spend our time, efforts and money, and how these elements interact with each other and the world around us.

From its earliest days, the discipline of economics has walked a fine line between focusing merely on how we allocate these resources, and a wider array of questions about how society works – and even how it should work. Aristotle wrote about economics in terms of organising stuff, but he threw in an ethical dimension, too. He talked about a 'just price' at which people should trade, and explored the notion that money for its own sake is a morally bad thing. He thought economics was a natural pursuit, an essential part of humans achieving their best, inherently good, nature. Almost two millennia later, Adam Smith, the grandfather of modern economics, wrote the foundational text of the discipline, *The Wealth of Nations*. He argued that when people follow their naked self-interest they could drive an efficient use of our resources and make us all better off. But Smith, too, was concerned by the moral dimension of the economy.[3] A few years earlier, he had written an equally important but less famous book, *The Theory of Moral Sentiments*, which highlighted the ethical and social questions at the core of his view of economics.

These competing visions of economics – one narrowly focused on resource allocation, the other a broader attempt to make sense of how society works – have long been debated by economists. John Maynard Keynes, one of the twentieth century's most influential thinkers, once said that the master economist must leave 'no part of man's nature or his institutions ... outside his regard'.[4] More recently, the University of Cambridge economist Diane Coyle has noted that there is an implicit and unavoidable moral framework underlying economics, especially when it comes to setting economic policy.[5]

This wider view of economics takes account of the fact that economics doesn't operate in a vacuum. Decisions on how to allocate the things that we have in the 'best' possible way require value judgements – they depend on what kind of society we want to aim for. Economics can inform that decision. Which means it is inherently linked to broader political and social questions. It is, in short, a *social* science.

At times in its history, some economists have tried to emphasise the 'science' part of that package. In the late nineteenth century, Alfred Marshall, the economist who tutored Keynes, began to lead the way in formalising economics. He wanted the discipline to be more of a hard science, and to move away from philosophical and moral debates.[6] Economists began crafting mathematical models full of equations, which attempted to distil how people make decisions and interact with each other – an approach more akin to physics than psychology or sociology. In some places, economics literally became rocket science: economists borrowed modelling techniques that were originally used to guide navigation systems on ballistic projectiles.[7] Perhaps tellingly, however, even before the end of his career, Marshall had come to view the use of mathematics in economics as at most a tool; he believed it should be used sparingly, and, at its worst, that it could be an active hindrance to economists. Still, the formalisation of economics that he set in motion outlived him and would become the dominant way of doing things for a century or so.

More recently, however, economics has become wider and more diverse. Fields such as behavioural economics have made links to other disciplines – pointing out that humans aren't coldly rational and calculating and in order to understand their economic behaviour you need to study the inner workings of their minds. Today's economists have started to incorporate ideas from sociology, psychology and even biology to achieve a more rounded view of the discipline: one that combines the scientific rigour sought by Marshall with the pluralistic ethos of Aristotle and Smith.

Where does that leave economics now? Modern economics has branched out into a wide array of specialised areas. Economists study financial markets, poverty, ecosystems, even well-being and happiness. Their research touches on how and why we work, what we spend, what we make, how we interact with other countries and the natural resources around us.

So economics matters. It matters not just to geeky economists sitting in dark rooms and crunching numbers. It matters for you and all of the people around you too. Most of the big questions that define our lives are informed by economics. Whether you were born into a rich country or a poor one, your standard of living will be determined by huge economic forces. Growth and its relationship with climate change are both questions built on economics, and economics has a lot to say about the best ways to address the escalating climate emergency, so that we can use the finite resources we have in an efficient and sustainable way.[8]

However, there are also smaller questions, closer to home. What determines how much of a pay rise you get, and how far your money goes each month? How do you decide between buying things now or saving for the future? These are questions that economics can help you answer.

All this means that understanding economics can have a huge impact on your life. Economics can make you happier, healthier and wealthier: economic literacy has been shown to improve your life expectancy, mental well-being and lifetime earnings, to name just a few benefits. This is something that most people understand intuitively. In the UK, over 80 per cent of people say that economics is relevant, or very relevant, to their everyday lives.[9] They get it. The fact that you've picked up this book means you probably get it too.

But there is a disconnect. People know they should understand economics, they want to understand economics – and yet they don't. A study in 2020 found that the average person has limited knowledge about how figures for basic economic indicators, such as unemployment and inflation, are collected and calculated.[10] Research by the Global Financial Literacy Excellence Center suggests only a third of people worldwide have basic financial literacy, and that this state of affairs is associated with negative outcomes such as low financial inclusion and people becoming disconnected from the financial world around them.[11] This is further borne out by surveys showing a significant majority of the public think that economics is inaccessible to them, even when it is being explained by savvy communicators like journalists or politicians.[12]

Economists probably don't help themselves here. The dependence on abstract models built on bizarre-sounding assumptions, often written in complex mathematical formulae, can make economics sound otherworldly – detached from the everyday home management that intrigued Aristotle. Economists have not always been the savviest of communicators, either. The former Chief Economist at the Bank of England, Andy Haldane, once said that 'an economist with strong social skills is one who stares at your shoes, rather than their own, when engaged in polite conversation'.[13]

We at the Bank of England have often been guilty of this ourselves. The Bank was founded in 1694 to 'promote the public good and benefit of our people', meaning, at the time, the people of England.[14] These lofty ideals were written into the original founding charter and sound slightly better than to 'help the King fund a war against the French', which might have been more honest.[15] This raison d'etre – the first one, not the second – remains at the core of the Bank's purpose to this day.

Yet for much of its history, the Bank was both integral to the British economy and opaque and distant from most people's economic lives. A former Bank Governor infamously once said that the Bank should 'never apologise, never explain' – not an ideal way to promote understanding.[16] And that is before we get to the incomprehensibly coded messages the Bank would sometimes use to communicate to those few in the know. In the City of London, some people even claimed to have been able to read messages about what would happen to the economy by watching the eyebrow movements of the Governor.

In these moments, we central bankers have perhaps failed in one of our longest-established duties. To effectively achieve our three-centuries-old objective, we must engage with the people we serve – and not just through eyebrow movements. That means looking up from our footwear and speaking to people on their terms, in ways that they find useful.

In recent years, the Bank has tried to make its explanations of its policy decisions more accessible. It has also tried to educate the public about economics: through an outreach programme in schools, by developing a host of online resources about the economy, and even by partnering with the *Beano* comic to develop an entertaining and playful way for young children (and some adults) to engage with economics. More recently, the Bank has been travelling across the UK to hold forums on what the public thinks about the economy – our attempt to get out of our silos, learn from people's economic experiences and see how much central bankers truly understand the economic forces that are important to their daily lives.[17]

This book aims to carry on that mission. It will walk you through some of the core economic concepts that shape the world around you. Each chapter attempts to answer a question that one of your authors has been asked by friends, family or members of the public since we joined the Bank: from why all our clothes are made abroad, to what on earth makes money into money.

We start broadly with what economists call 'microeconomics', which relates to the decisions taken by individual people and individual businesses. You'll learn what markets are and how they determine the prices of the things you buy and sell. Then we'll turn to the circumstances in which markets don't work, leading on to problems caused by everything from monopolies to climate change. Next, we'll examine how economists think about work, and how the forces affecting the labour market lead to unemployment even in growing, affluent economies.

This same chapter marks a transition into what economists call 'macroeconomics', which looks at economies as entire systems, the result of those individual decisions being brought together. We'll explain economic growth: how a combination of natural resources, people, machines and know-how come together to create what we measure as economic output, and how this has raised the standards of living of people globally throughout time. You'll encounter the underlying reasons why nations trade with one another, and how that can make the whole world better off. Then we'll turn to inflation, the process by which our money gradually erodes in value – and why that might not always be a bad thing.

Next, you'll learn about the money in your pocket. Hopefully you'll come to see that it is not just a piece of metal or plastic; it's much more than that – it's a system of social trust that is one of the most enduring institutions in human history. From there, we'll introduce you to the role of banks – including central banks, like the Bank of

England – in making the economy run smoothly. However, things don't always go as smoothly as we might hope, so in the penultimate chapter we'll introduce you to some major economic crises that have occurred and explain how they came about. Finally, in the last chapter you'll learn about the levers that policymaking institutions – like the Bank of England, other central banks and governments – can pull to help the economy keep ticking over. At the end of the book, we've included an appendix that identifies where to turn if you have a more specific question about the economy (and want an answer right away).

Why should you trust us to teach you? Well, we, your authors, are economists at the Bank of England. Between us we have spent decades studying the intricacies of economics and applying what we've learned to some of the biggest questions of recent years, from Brexit to Covid-19.[18] We've also spent a long time thinking about how best to communicate these ideas to as broad an audience as possible, whether via the Bank's schools outreach programmes or in its blog pages. We haven't written this book alone, however. It has drawn on the knowledge of dozens of economists across the Bank. The chapters have been drafted in consultation with specialist policymakers, and we have incorporated feedback from experts on everything from inflation to growth, unemployment to monetary policy. The result is a book that is, fingers crossed, both authoritative and readable.

Our hope is that by the time you finish this book you will be better able to make sense of the economic world you inhabit. That might be as simple as feeling confident enough to pipe up in a conversation about inflation or interest rates at the pub, or being able to explain to your boss why you deserve a bigger pay rise, or feeling empowered to engage more deeply with the big debates of our time, whether on climate change or GDP.

Economics isn't everything, but it almost is. Especially if done properly. So a world in which a few more of us understand economics can only be a better one, right?

Chapter One
Where does my breakfast come from?

On supply and demand, the (sometimes) magical power of markets, and why Woolworths' Pic'n'Mix was the start of your economic education.

It's a Saturday morning and you are going to meet some friends for breakfast. The choice is dazzling. You could go to a greasy spoon and buy a disconcertingly cheap fry-up. You could nip into a Greggs and buy a breakfast bap then sit down to eat it on a park bench. Or you could head to a local artisanal coffee shop and buy the supposed staple breakfast of the urban millennial: smashed avocado on toast.

Do you ever wonder where all these breakfast options have come from? How is it that this abstract thing we call 'the economy' manages to offer us such a dizzying array of things to consume – eggs, baps, avocados? How does all this stuff manage to get to you from around the world, so that at the precise moment you want your breakfast there's an array of options right there in your home town? And how is it possible for all this to happen so cheaply – at a price that you and all your friends can justify to yourselves?

These are, perhaps, the foundational questions of economics. In a world of scarce resources, how do we make sure that the stuff we need or want gets to us when we need and want it? The economist's answer relates to markets: the interplay of people and organisations, and the way they come together to bring us all the panoply of goods, services and prices that we see around us all the time.

At the heart of that process there is you and your fry-up, breakfast bap or avocado on toast. You are an integral part of the economy. If we want to understand where your breakfast comes from, we need to start with the economics of your choices.

Every single day you make dozens, if not hundreds, of decisions. Some may seem small: do I buy a bagel for lunch or make a salad at home? Do I take the bus or drive? Others might be larger: do I apply for a new job or not? Do I save for a deposit on a house or buy a few extra avocado breakfasts?[1]

Why do you need to make so many decisions? Because we live in a finite world in which we cannot have and do everything. We are constantly coming up against constraints that hold back our desires. These may be constraints on how much money we have to spend – budget constraints. They may be constraints on the physical and natural materials that we can draw on – resource constraints. Or it may just be that there are only so many hours in the day – time constraints.

Often these decisions interact in complicated ways. Consider your decisions as a worker: do you prioritise work or play? Working will earn you more money, easing the budget constraint and increasing the options you have to buy things, but it also eats away at your time constraint. The more hours you spend working, the fewer there are to enjoy the fruits of that labour.

Or consider your decisions as a consumer. Do you spend all of your money, or do you put some away for a rainy day? If the latter, how much do you save? And for how long? If you spend it, do you buy the blue dress or the red dress? Peanut butter or chocolate spread? Coke or Pepsi? Fry-up or avocado on toast? Depending on the choices you make, you may need to work more, or even change jobs, in order to be able to fund them.

To see how these decisions play out in practice, come with us back to early 2009, to the moment when a century-long era ended. On 21 February 2009, the very last Woolworths' Pic'n'Mix was sold – for an eye-watering £14,500. For those who remember the joy of heading down to the local high street and spending your weekly allowance on sugar and E-numbers, this was a sad day. Over the previous century, the Woolworths' Pic'n'Mix had become a cultural icon in the United Kingdom and around the world. A wall of sweets of all sizes and colours – fizzy cola bottles, jelly beans, chocolate buttons. It was the closest most of us ever got to Willy Wonka's Chocolate Factory outside of the pages of a book.

Amidst the sugar rush of all those sweets, you may not have realised you were actually illustrating the perfect microcosm of consumer behaviour. You had a budget constraint, which was however much money you had managed to earn/charm/extort out of your family and friends. You had a whole series of options to spend it on – the sweets. And you had your own personal preferences. Some people may have decided that their preference for cola bottles was so strong that they would use their entire allowance on a bag of those. For some, they might have been tempted by chocolate-covered raisins. But for most it was likely to be a mix of a lot of things, with more weight given to their favourite sweets.

Given you only had a certain amount to spend, you would have been likely to come up against a trade-off. The Pic'n'Mix's price was calculated by weight. If a sweet was heavy – say a gobstopper – did you prefer one of those, or three of the lighter sweets? When your bag was too heavy, you would have to choose to put something back. It probably wouldn't be the sweet you only had one of – better to put back one of the sweets you had twenty of already. Unconsciously, everybody faced with the Pic'n'Mix wall was confronted with the same challenge: weighing up trade-offs in light of their preferences.

Every day we bring together our preferences with our various constraints and we decide what it is we want to spend our money, our time and our efforts on. And what is your guiding principle in making that decision? Subject to all the various constraints, you want to get the most out of it – to live your best life. Economists tend to assume that the basis of consumers' decision-making is that each of us is trying to get the most benefit out of the resources we have.

This idea is encapsulated in a slightly abstract concept: 'utility'. Sometimes defined as the pleasure, satisfaction or benefit you get from doing or consuming things, utility can be anything you value: from a new outfit that makes you look and feel good to the sensation of not being hungry once you've eaten a burger. According to economics, utility is something you want to maximise. This is precisely what you were trying to do as you weighed up your Pic'n'Mix choices: you get different levels of enjoyment from the various combinations of sweets, and so you value them differently.

This idea – 'utility maximisation' – can feel slightly detached. The utility you get from work is not just about how much money you make – although that might be part of the picture. It is about the enjoyment, the stimulation, the sense of feeling worthwhile. So when you see someone taking a job that pays less money than they could be earning elsewhere, it is not a failure of the basic economic model, it simply means they get more utility – more benefit – from their new job, having taken a wider array of factors into account. Ultimately, this basic economic model is built on every individual looking to maximise their own utility through a series of trade-offs.

In practice, that means thinking about what something costs. These costs can take many forms. There is obviously a monetary cost to buying something – its price – and prices are often closely related to utility. The more utility you get from something, the more you would be willing to pay for it, and therefore the price you agree on can be seen as a signal of the utility gain.

But this is not the only kind of cost. Economists think about cost in a slightly different way, one that captures more than just the money you're handing over. They often talk about opportunity costs. In this framing, the cost of something is not just what you pay, but what you give up or lose by choosing one option over another. For example, paying a hairdresser to cut your hair costs more than cutting it yourself, but what about the time you have to give up to do it? You might take twice as long as a skilled hairdresser, and that is time you could have spent doing something else. Cutting your own hair has come at the cost of whatever else you could have been doing with that time. And what if your amateur attempts to cut your own hair, however heroic, mean that you're not taken seriously in a job interview and you don't get the job you would have got if you had had a swish, professional-looking barnet? Now the opportunity cost of cutting your own hair seems huge and really not worth it.

The journalist and author Tim Harford offers a useful description about how thinking in terms of opportunity cost can improve almost all of the decisions we make in life – particularly for those of us who tend to find it hard to say no to things.[2] He suggests flipping around the choices you are given: instead of considering what you are saying 'yes' to when you agree to something, think about what you are saying 'no' to – the opportunity cost. Saying yes to staying late at work means saying no to reading your daughter a bedtime story; saying yes to that extra drink in happy hour means saying no to the early morning run, and a clear head the next day.

These opportunity costs are a ubiquitous feature of the economy. People often talk about a 'false economy' of going for cheaper items, or say that a more expensive product 'pays for itself' in the opportunities it presents. This is everyday opportunity cost. It will be mentioned time and time again throughout this book in all kinds of situations; from the opportunity cost of going to university (or not), to the opportunity cost of focusing on doing a job you're bad at when you could be focusing on one that you're good at.

The result of all these choices and trade-offs is that you ultimately decide how much of each thing you want: how large your demand for it is. You are exercising this demand every time you decide what breakfast to buy, or whether to skip breakfast altogether. Demand is one of the building blocks of economics. And the starting point for making sense of demand in an economy is a rule called, uncreatively, the law of demand.

The law of demand is about as close to a universal law as the world of economics has. It states that as something becomes more expensive we want less of it, and as it becomes cheaper we want more of it. It is why companies cut prices in the sales when they have excess stock they need to sell. It is a rarity in economics – intuitively correct, but also backed up by a wealth of data and theoretical research.

Take happy hour in your local pub. Happy hour discounts invariably come early in the evening, before the time when people really want to go big on their drinking. Yet more than 60 per cent of bars' alcohol sales can come from happy hour periods.[3] Why? The drinks are exactly the same, and the preferences of punters haven't changed.

What has changed is the price. Happy hour makes drinks cheaper and, as the law of demand would indicate, that makes us want more of them. This is the same reason why Amazon sells significantly more Echo Dots on its heavily discounted Prime Day than on other days, despite the product on offer being the same.

Economists tend to break this phenomenon down into two distinct elements. First, the lower price means you can buy more of the product. You are relatively richer than you were with a higher price – your £10 gets you three beers, not two.[4] This is called the income effect. Second, the thing you're buying is now cheaper relative to other things, so it becomes more attractive. So you substitute away from other things. In our happy hour example, this could be a switch from choosing drinks not covered by the happy hour deal – cocktails instead of sauvignon – or, perhaps more worryingly, a switch from buying drinks in the future to buying more of them now. We've all witnessed that run to the bar at two minutes to the end of happy hour – what those people are doing is substituting a relatively more expensive drink in the future for a relatively cheaper drink now. This switching from other things when something becomes relatively cheaper is known as the substitution effect.

While this law of demand generally holds true, it can play out very differently depending on what's being bought or sold. For some goods, a small shift in the price can lead to big swings in how much you want. For others, the price may move drastically and it has little or no impact on your decision over how much to buy. This sensitivity of how much you want to buy to a change in price is called the 'price elasticity of demand'.

Consider plastic carrier bags. In 2010, the devolved Welsh government announced a charge for carrier bags that had, until that moment, largely been given away for free. They were subsequently followed by the administrations of Northern Ireland, Scotland and, eventually, England. The aim was to discourage people from using carrier bags and reduce the negative impact that single-use plastic has on the environment. But the increase in price was relatively small, at least in absolute terms – from nothing to 5p. What the various governments were hoping was that demand for carrier bags was particularly sensitive to prices. And they were right; even a small increase managed to reduce usage of single-use bags by over 90 per cent, and all types of bags, including the optimistically named 'bag for life', fell by more than 20 per cent.[5]

On the other hand, imagine there was a parasite that threatened to crawl inside your brain and leave you blind and paralysed, perhaps even kill you. Fortunately, there is a drug that can safely neutralise the parasite and protect you. How much would you be willing to pay for that drug? Probably quite a lot. That, at least, was the judgement of Martin Shkreli, the former CEO of Turing Pharmaceuticals. Shkreli – who became known as the 'Pharma Bro' – cranked up the price of Daraprim, a drug that protected people with vulnerable immune systems from the toxoplasma parasite, from $13 to $750.[6] He was counting on the fact that people's demand was not very sensitive to the price and that they would still want a similar amount of the drug even at a hugely inflated price. As it turned out, Shkreli had misjudged the market: the public backlash and the development of a cheaper alternative meant that within a few years Turing's sales had fallen, and with them its profit. However, less extreme examples of inelastic demand often see price rises that don't lead to a notable fall in demand. How much would the price of petrol have to go up before you decided to drive to work less and use less petrol?

This sort of inelastic demand can also result from something having addictive properties. The classic example is cigarettes. Anyone who has felt the cravings of early-stage nicotine withdrawal will tell you that in that moment you're less likely to quibble over an extra 50p to secure your next hit. A study in 2013 found that for every 1 per cent increase in the price of cigarettes, demand fell by as little as a third of 1 per cent.[7] That means that for the average pack of twenty in the UK a 10 per cent increase – roughly £1 more per packet – would reduce demand by 3 per cent, or less than one cigarette in the pack.

The law of demand isn't the be-all and end-all, however. Some forces that don't relate to price can drive increases or decreases in demand. Here, too, smoking is an illustrative example. The mid-1960s marked the peak of cigarette demand, at least in the United States. In 1963, around 40 per cent of the US adult population smoked – in fact, they smoked enough for every adult to have more than half a packet each and every day.[8] Cigarette smoking was also deemed to be cool. Some of the hippest celebrities of the age would smoke publicly and profusely – think of John Wayne, with a cigarette dangling from his mouth in every Western, or the 'Rat Pack' singers, made up of the heavy smokers Frank Sinatra,

Sammy Davis Jr. and Dean Martin. So, naturally, cigarette demand was high.

Since the 1960s, we've become much more aware of the health risks of smoking. Public policy campaigns have emphasised the negatives and shifted the tone. There may still be parts of society where smoking is considered cool, but in general, society's perception of cigarettes has changed. Recent survey evidence from secondary school pupils in England (mostly aged 11 to 15) showed that 19 per cent had tried smoking at least once – a shocking stat until you learn that thirty years ago this number was close to 50 per cent. The trend is similar for regular smokers: in 2016, only 3 per cent of children that age were regular smokers, compared to 10 per cent thirty years ago.[9] This change in tastes and fashions has led to a consistent decline in the demand for cigarettes for over half a century. In the UK, demand fell by 25 per cent between 2011 and 2018 – representing almost 25 billion fewer cigarettes being smoked.[10]

All this shows that price isn't everything.[11] Changes in tastes, fashions and preferences are fluid and will always lead to shifts in demand – rising if a product has been endorsed by a celebrity, falling if it's been cancelled on social media, for example. Likewise, as people become more aware of the ethical and environmental impact of their consumption, demand for products deemed unethical or environmentally damaging declines.

How much you earn also shifts your demand. This can be in an absolute sense – as you get more money your budget constraint is relaxed, you have more to spend, and so you are likely to spend more than you did before (even on goods you once deemed too expensive). But it can also be true in a relative sense. As countries become richer they have tended to consume more meat – in absolute terms, but also as a proportion of people's income. In 1961, China consumed less than 4kg of meat per person per year, with it being a rarity for many.[12] Today, the figure is closer to 63kg, a much higher fraction of the average Chinese income and gaining ground on the share spent in countries like the US and UK.[13]

Finally, some forces that cause changes in demand having nothing to do with the actual product in question. Consider the world's favourite fizzy drink. When the price of Coca-Cola goes up, what would you expect to happen to demand for Pepsi? For some diehard aficionados, their brand is their brand – nothing could make them switch. But for many, if Coke became more expensive they would switch to Pepsi. Think back to the substitution effect in our happy hour example; Coke and Pepsi are substitutes, so if one goes up in price, people swap over to the other. This impact of the price of one thing that's on demand for another is known as 'cross-elasticity'.

In the case of substitutes, such as Coca-Cola and Pepsi, this cross-elasticity is a positive number: meaning that as the price of one thing goes up, the demand for the other thing also goes up. For some items, though, this cross-elasticity is a negative number: as the price of one goes up, we demand less of something else. Think about what happens to demand for Xbox games when the price of an Xbox goes up, or the demand for doughnuts when the price of coffee increases. These products are called complements: having one is linked to having the other, so if the price of one goes up and you buy less of it, you also buy less of the other.

In all of these instances, though, it is usually safe to say that the law of demand still holds true. However fashionable an influencer-endorsed cleaning brand becomes, as it gets more expensive people will start to look elsewhere. However high your salary goes, if you have the choice between two identical pints of milk you would most likely go for the cheaper one. When Coke's price goes up, people buy Pepsi instead. Demand is affected by price – and, as a general rule, the cheaper the goods the more of it people want.

But the law of demand doesn't always hold up. In a few cases, increasing the price of something actually makes people want *more* of it. One reason for this might simply be showing off. Think back to the last time you were at a restaurant. Your date is sat opposite you and the waiter comes over and offers you the wine list. What do you order? You might think about what matches best with your food, contemplating the provenance of the grape varieties on offer and the climatic conditions in the specific years mentioned. Or, if you're like at least 21 per cent of the population, you will go for the second-cheapest wine on the list because you don't want to appear cheap, but you also don't know or care enough about wine to go for an expensive one.[14] In this case, the law of demand has failed us: if the second-cheapest wine was reduced in price to cost less than the cheapest wine, you would demand less of it. Being more expensive actually makes you want more.

Perhaps ordering the second-cheapest bottle of wine isn't quite the height of luxury, but the same principle applies to a whole variety of luxury items, from sports cars to fine art. People value the signal that buying something expensive sends to the world around them, so the higher the price, the better. In 1899, the American economist Thorstein Veblen named this phenomenon 'conspicuous consumption', and goods that obeyed this rule became known as Veblen goods.

A less glamorous violation of the law of demand was spotted some years earlier by the Scottish economist Robert Giffen.[15] From his observations on Victorian Britain, Giffen noticed that as the price of bread went up, poor families living in city slums demanded more of it. It was a peculiar result. Why would the poorest people in the country want more of something as it gets more expensive? Unlike with Veblen's process, this had nothing to do with showing off. Rather, they were splitting their income between something essential – bread – and something more luxurious – like meat. When the price of bread went up, the families no longer had enough money left from buying the essential (bread) to buy the luxury (meat). They doubled down and spent their change on more bread than before.

Products that followed this tendency became known as Giffen goods. They are still with us, although they are more of a rarity than in the nineteenth century. In 2008 American economists Robert Jensen and Nolan Miller conducted a detailed study of the demand for rice in China and found that it displayed the same properties as Giffen had outlined for bread in Victorian Britain.[16]

So that's demand: the result of your choices as a consumer and a worker, balancing a whole host of trade-offs and then scaled up across an entire economy. But you are not alone. There are other economic actors out there, tasked with supplying the things we want. That's where firms come in.

In economics, a firm is a group of people who come together to create something to sell. To do so, they draw on a variety of 'inputs': workers, machines, raw materials. Firms can take many forms; from a huge mining firm needing drills, land and technicians to create iron ore, to an entrepreneurial knitter bringing together a needle and some wool to knit a jumper and sell it on eBay, to an artisanal bakery that's offering you that delicious combination of avocado and toasted bread.

Just like consumers, firms – or businesses, as we will call them from now on – have to make decisions: what to produce, how much of it to produce, and at what price to sell it. The working assumption in economics is that the end goal of any business is to make as much money as possible. Or, to be precise, to maximise their profits – that is, the money left over when all of their costs have been paid.

But how does a business maximise its profits? It's a question that many business owners have pondered. The economist's answer is to keep on producing more, until the cost of producing just one more thing outweighs the additional revenue you would get from selling it. Then you stop.

The impact of producing just one more thing is known as the marginal impact, and it is a useful concept for economists and businesses alike. To get a clearer sense of the impact it has, let's imagine you're running a T-shirt company. You sell 100 T-shirts at £20 each and they cost you

£15 to make. So you're taking in £2,000 and your costs are £1,500. You are making a profit of £500.

Now, imagine you decide to produce one more T-shirt: tee number 101. To be able to sell that T-shirt, you need to entice someone who wouldn't have bought one before. So you drop the price to £19.99. Your revenue has now gone up to around £2,019. Importantly, you have had to drop the price of all your tees, not just the extra one. This means your 'marginal revenue' for the extra tee is £19. If your costs don't change, the 'marginal cost' of one more tee is £15. Your profits will increase by £4. The extra revenue you get for producing one more tee is higher than the extra cost. So you should do it.

So far so good. But what about producing 102 tees? Well, to sell that tee you would need to drop the price from £19.99 to £19.90. Your marginal revenue still increases, this time by £10. This might seem counterintuitive, given you are selling the tee for £19.90, but remember, you've also had to cut the price on the other 101 tees you are selling. This marginal revenue of £10 is now less than the marginal cost of producing tee number 102, which is £15. Even though £19.90 is more than £15, by producing tee 102 you are actually adding more to your costs than you are getting for it, compared to just producing 101. You shouldn't do it.

This process means that, if a business is acting completely rationally, it will keep on producing stuff until its marginal revenue exactly matches its marginal cost. This is where your profit is highest. Produce less and you're missing out on extra profit, produce more and you are reducing your profit unnecessarily.

For some, this pursuit of profit above all else may seem distasteful. In an economic sense, however, it is often an efficient way of motivating businesses to produce what consumers want. In fact, according to some economists, companies' pursuit of profit isn't just efficient – it's a moral duty. Milton Friedman, one of the twentieth century's most influential economists, wrote a famous article in the *New York Times* in 1970, with an eye-catching title: 'The Social Responsibility Of Business Is to Increase Its Profits'.[17]

His argument was that if individuals in society valued socially responsible production they would choose to spend their money on things that were produced in a socially responsible way. If lots of people valued climate-friendly activities, they would choose to spend their money on them. If individuals didn't value those things enough to spend their own money on them, then what right did companies have to make that decision for them? It wasn't the place of businesses to make these calls. If they did, Friedman argued, it was harmful. By choosing to do something 'ethical' that made them less money, they were ultimately taking money out of the pockets of the company's shareholders and workers – and that meant less money for those people to spend on the things that they, as individuals, actually valued. This analysis became known as the Friedman Doctrine.

Unsurprisingly, this was a controversial argument. Since the Friedman Doctrine was outlined, it has been critiqued on many grounds – not least its notion that individuals have enough information and power to make good decisions about what it is 'ethical' to buy. It also sits at odds with the modern trend for corporate social responsibility. In the real world, companies and businesses aren't just soulless profit-seeking machines – at least, not all of them are. Today, many businesses put ethical and environmental concerns at the heart of their decision-making, saying this is as important as straightforwardly aiming to grow their profits. (Of course, a more cynical reader might say that this too is in part about profit maximisation – with companies trying to win round customers who increasingly value moral credentials by presenting themselves as more ethical than their competitors.)

But the Friedman Doctrine, under which every business ruthlessly pursues profit above all else, remains the most common distillation of how the economists' model of society works. Every business keeps producing stuff, until doing so starts to eat away at its profits. As a result, everyone in society benefits.

Whatever their motives, businesses provide us with the things that we want to buy. They organise the supply of goods and services to the economy. And, as with demand, supply has its own law.

The law of supply is the mirror image of the law of demand. As the price goes up, businesses will want to provide more of it; as the price goes down, businesses will want to provide less. As with demand, this is intuitive. At a low price, it might be very hard to make much money selling something. The costs might even mean it wouldn't be profitable to produce it. However, as the price goes up, more of these companies that weren't profitable suddenly become viable.

You can see this process in action if you look at the market for shale oil and gas. Scientists have long known that oil and natural gas are present in a type of rock known as shale, but until recently they didn't have the technology to extract it easily. That all changed in the 1990s and 2000s. Technical innovations meant that it became possible to extract shale oil and gas by mixing water, sand and chemicals at high pressure and pumping it into the ground. This process is technologically savvy, but it certainly isn't cheap. Such shale rigs are costly to run, so many aren't profitable if the price of oil is below $40 or $50 a barrel.[18] In recent years, whenever the price of oil has increased above that threshold, there has been a noticeable increase in the number of working shale rigs, boosting the supply of oil and gas in response to the higher price. It's the law of supply in action.

As with its counterpart law of demand, the supply of some things is more sensitive, or elastic, to price changes than others. Take the experience of England's football fans in 2021. On Sunday 11 July 2021, Wembley Stadium in London hosted the final of the Covid-postponed Euro 2020 football competition: England's first final in a major tournament since 1966. Those who had bought tickets for the match well in advance were likely to have paid around £250 for a standard seat. But when England made it to the final, demand for tickets surged. England, it must be admitted, don't get into many finals. This could have been a once-in-a-lifetime opportunity.

The problem was, there was no way for supply to respond to the increase in demand. There is only one Wembley Stadium – it can hold no more than 90,000 people at the best of times, and it could only take 67,000 in summer 2021 (when restrictions arising from the Covid-19 pandemic were still in place). This meant that however much the price went up, no business could produce more tickets. The supply of seats at that match was almost perfectly inelastic, insensitive to even huge price rises. And huge price rises there were. The ticket touts – an industry with a canny understanding of the inelastic nature of supply, especially when they help control it – were eventually charging as much as £35,000 per ticket: a price increase of almost 14,000 per cent.[19]

This is an extreme example, but more everyday instances of inelastic forms of supply are everywhere. The writer Mark Twain is said to have once quipped that people should buy land: 'they aren't making it any more'. It wouldn't have been a surprise to Twain that the value of land has increased more than fifty times over in the 100 or so years since, far outstripping the average increase in other products.

And as with the law of demand, price isn't the only factor informing how much stuff gets made. Many forces beyond demand can shape the amount that businesses are willing to produce and supply. If the prices of a business's inputs goes down – workers become cheaper to hire, for example – then they'll get more profit for the same selling price and choose to supply more. If your bar owner gets a discount on some bottles of beer that are close to their expiry date, but the price they can sell them for is the same, they are going to want to supply more than they did before.

*

So we've met demand and supply, consumers and businesses. But there's something missing in our explanation; the place where supply and demand meet. This is where prices are determined. This is where the real magic happens: markets.

The word market conjures up mental images of chipper cockney stall-owners in Albert Square. This is certainly part of it. For economists, however, a market is nothing more than a place where buyers meet sellers. That could be a market stall in Walford, or an auction house selling fine art to dealers. It could be stockbrokers yelling at each other on a trading floor in the City of London, or a *Bake Off*-inspired entrepreneur selling homemade biscuits to cookie-lovers on the internet. There are markets for luxury, markets for labour, even markets for love.[20] Put simply, a market is anywhere buyers and sellers come together to agree how much, and at what price. They are the place where demand meets supply.

How do these markets work in practice? An extreme and tragic example came in 2014 in Sydney, Australia. On the morning of 15 December, a gunman took members of the public hostage in a cafe in the central business district. Panic ensued. As people tried to flee the centre of the city and return to their homes, many turned to their phones and tried to pick up an Uber. But they were surprised by what they found – prices had rocketed to eye-watering levels. In the days that followed there was public outcry and significant backlash against Uber, who ultimately refunded fares for all those fleeing attacks. However, the horrifying incident provided a powerful, if disturbing, example of how markets work – the inexorable outcome of the laws of supply and demand.

Uber's price structure is based on an algorithm that had calculated the supply of drivers in the area, the demand for those drivers, then found a price that balanced the two. If there were lots of drivers with nothing to do, the app lowered the price until a few more people decided it was cheap enough to justify hailing an Uber. If, as was the case in Sydney in 2014, there were more people wanting a lift than there were drivers willing to give them one, the algorithm bumped up the price. Doing this would have two effects. First, it would make it more attractive for Uber drivers to come to the area, increasing the supply. A driver planning to break for lunch might decide it was now worthwhile to take one more fare before stopping for a sandwich. Second, it would make some people think twice about hailing a car, reducing demand. As the price continues to go up, more people get priced out, or decide to walk instead – and more drivers decide it is a good idea to get a piece of the action. In the end, the number of drivers will match the number of people wanting lifts.

Uber's surge-pricing algorithm reflects how markets bring supply and demand into balance. What happens if, at a given price, people want to buy more than businesses are willing to sell? Markets, like most economists, like balance, and markets have an in-built mechanism for achieving that balance – or equilibrium, as economists refer to it.

If more people want to buy than want to sell at the price on offer, demand is greater than supply. Someone is going to get left out, and no one wants to be that person. That means those who can afford to do so will offer a little bit more – to ensure they get the amount they want. The increased price then means that some people are priced out, or decide they aren't willing to pay that much, and so demand falls. Then, seeing the opportunity for a bit of additional profit, some businesses may start to increase their supply. This process guides the price up until supply and demand are once again in balance.

When it works, this is an enchanting process: with the interplay of supply and demand ultimately meaning that everyone gets access to the things they need most – in theory, at least. Prices, in this telling, are a type of signal – communicating to producers if they should make more of something, or less. Prices going up mean that demand is going up relative to supply, so businesses should create more. Prices going down is a signal that supply is going up relative to demand, so businesses should create less. The effects of these signals can be extraordinary. Arising from the countless decisions that all of us make every day, they unleash one of the most powerful forces in the history of the world – the force of the market.

So what did you have for breakfast this morning? A fry-up? A breakfast bap? A rushed cup of black coffee before you ran for the bus? Let's say you went for our by-now-familiar avocado on toast. Take a moment to think about what had to happen for it to be there just when you wanted it.

Months before you sat down to eat it, someone halfway around the world had to decide to plant the seeds and tend to them to grow the avocados. Someone else in another part of the world was growing the wheat that would eventually become your sourdough toast. That's not to mention the lorry drivers who brought the avocados to where you live, or the bakers who cooked the bread. The number of steps and processes and people involved in making your breakfast a reality is incredible.

But what's more incredible is that no one organises it. There is no central, controlling authority telling people how many avocados to plant and how much to sell them for. The vast majority of the people involved in creating your breakfast have never met one another.

Even more remarkably, none of them even really cares about your breakfast personally – they are creating it because it's in their interest to do so. As the founder of modern economics, Adam Smith, put it, 'it is not by the benevolence of the butcher, of the baker that we expect them to provide our food, but their own self-interest'.[21] Smith called this process the 'invisible hand' of the market. Smith's thesis was that, on the whole, this invisible hand led individuals to do what was best for society as a whole, producing what was desired efficiently.

That avocado grower isn't producing fresh green produce because she feels an obligation to you. She almost certainly has never and will never meet you. She is guided by the fact that, in doing so, she can gain utility (financial or otherwise). If she got more utility from producing something else, then she would likely produce that instead. And as we've seen, if there is an insufficient amount of something that people want, the price goes up until more of that thing is supplied. In this way, markets produce the things that people want, almost by magic.

Today, markets are the dominant mechanism organising global economies. Other ways of running economies have been tried – most famously in Communist regimes like the USSR and the German Democratic Republic, which shunned markets in favour of a state allocation of resources. But these systems struggled to internalise the millions – billions – of individual choices that the market does naturally. Over time, the global consensus has shifted in favour of using markets in at least some sectors of society and with some oversight. These markets, it seems, are just more efficient – approximating the collective will of everybody in an economy's choices. They are the reason your breakfast is right there, on time, at a good price.

Or that's the theory, at least. It doesn't take long to spot situations where markets are delivering outcomes that, as societies, we see as less than perfect: markets that feed an unsustainable demand for burning fossil fuels (or watering avocados); markets that lead to big, dominant businesses being able to exert massive power; and markets that reward those with an inside edge on information at the expense of those kept in the dark.

Economists are all too aware of this phenomenon. Even Adam Smith recognised that there are some situations in which markets end up working against the common good. It is the various failings of markets to which we now turn.

Chapter Two
Can economics solve climate change?

On the theory of perfect competition, how and why markets fail, and why economists always take too many chips.

On the top floor of the Bank of England's headquarters in London is the staff canteen. In times gone by, the Bank's offering to staff included an on-site wine bar, a restaurant, even a pub. Those halcyon days are long past. Nowadays, the Bank's top storey looks like many other staff canteens around the world. It sells all the things one would expect: sandwiches, salads and, most importantly, chips. Platefuls of them.

Every day, lines of hungry economists shuffle past a huge tray of piping-hot fried potatoes and shovel them onto their plates. It is the fuel that powers them through long afternoons of crunching numbers and writing reports. For this short portion of their day, they can switch off their brains and detach from the world of economics.

But if they didn't, they might have noticed that even here there are economic forces at play. Until recently, the Bank canteen charged one single price for chips, no matter how many you took. Yet the canteen staff had noticed a problem. People were taking far bigger portions than they needed to, leading to significant food waste from unfinished plates. At the same time, on some days there was a shortage of chips for those turning up late to the lunch hall.

The reason is not just that economists are greedy – although some undoubtedly are (we name no names). This is a well-documented problem in buffets around the world. It's down to what happens when there is a common resource, with lots of individuals each looking to get as much as they can personally. In these circumstances, every individual will tend to overconsume the resource – and unwittingly deplete, damage or destroy it.

In the 1960s, an economist and ecologist named Garrett Hardin described this phenomenon and named it the Tragedy of the Commons. He explained it using the example of common land, which was land owned by everyone in a village and used by them to rear animals. Each individual had an incentive to increase the number of animals they had on the land, because it would increase their income. But they do not take account of the fact that if everyone did this the land would become overused, degraded and eventually useless to everyone. As Hardin put it: 'Each man is locked into a system that compels him to increase his herd without limit, in a world that is limited.'[1] In the Bank of England's case, each economist is locked into a system that compels them to take too many chips, in a canteen of limited chip-pans.

This seems to cut against the dynamic described in Chapter One. There, we explored the potentially awesome power of markets in efficiently organising the world's resources. If people and businesses act rationally, trying to maximise their utility and profits, then in many cases everyone is better off – and everyone gets the stuff they need to live well. But phenomena like the Tragedy of the Commons reveal that, in some cases, this doesn't work out. Markets have limits. In places like the Bank of England canteen, everyone is acting entirely rationally, to maximise their potato-induced utility, and yet the collective outcome is not more efficiency, but less. Economists call these instances moments of 'market failure'.

Market failures are everywhere. They explain why, instead of using dozens of competing social networks, so many people just use Facebook. They explain why we might want the state to provide education for free, rather than everyone just buying and selling it on the market. And, as we'll see, they help to explain why the planet is facing a climate emergency – and what we might do in response.

Economists love models. To an economist, a model is anything used to represent and distil the complex reality we study into something useful. It could be lines on a graph, a set of equations, or nothing more than a series of logical arguments. The statistician George Box once said that 'all models are wrong, but some are useful'. His point was that all models make a set of assumptions to simplify the world around us; if they didn't, they would in effect *be* the world around us (and so wouldn't be much help in trying to understand it). The key, then, is to make sure that the simplifying assumptions you are making do not affect the answer to the question you are asking. In Box's words, you should ask not 'is the model true? (it never is) but is it good enough for this particular application?'[2]

Box's insight is one that both economists and critics of economists are sometimes guilty of forgetting. Their models are never right (as some economists might forget); but sometimes they are still useful (as some of their critics might ignore). His analysis is particularly informative when we are thinking about markets. Fledgling economists tend to start their modelling of markets and market processes with the assumption of 'perfect competition'. It rests on a number of assumptions that, taken together, may seem pretty unrealistic. The idea is not that the model represents how the world *really* works, outside of a relatively limited number of cases. Instead, it is your first building block when it comes to making sense of the economy. It's not perfect, but as the surrealist painter Salvador Dalí is reported to have said, you should 'have no fear of perfection – you'll never reach it'.

That's why these imperfect models are useful: thinking about why the real world falls short of perfection can help us to make sense of it.

A perfectly competitive market is one in which a number of conditions are met. First, all the sellers are selling the same, identical thing. Economists call this thing a homogenous good, which means that there are no distinguishing features between what one business and another is selling. That means no branding, and no differences in quality. Second, there must be a large number of buyers and sellers in the market, and there can be nothing stopping a new seller setting up and coming in should they want to – there are no 'barriers to entry'. Third, the buyers and sellers must be all-knowing. They know the quality of the goods they're buying, the approximate demand and supply for them, and the prices of all the alternative options. No one has an informational advantage compared with anyone else.

A market in which all of these conditions were met would have some interesting characteristics. For a start, no single seller or buyer would be able to affect the price. Everyone is what is known as a 'price taker'. That price is set at the point of minimum acceptable profit to all of the sellers: enough that they stay in profit, but not much more.

To see how this works, imagine that a business selling digestive biscuits decides to increase the price it charges. All the buyers in that market know that they can get an identical pack of digestive biscuits from an infinite number of other sellers. And those other sellers know that if they keep their price at the original level, they will steal the business from the seller who raised theirs. What's more, even if all the existing sellers decided to raise their price simultaneously, a canny biscuit entrepreneur could come in and steal everyone else's business by offering digestives at the original price – there are no barriers to entry, after all. This competitive dynamic would keep businesses honest, and would mean that the price settles at the point where businesses make just enough profit to make it worth their while.

When a market is in a state of perfect competition it is described as 'efficient'. Economists can mean a few different things when they call something efficient. For perfect competition, they are referring to two specific concepts. On the one hand, the market is 'productively efficient'. The product is being produced at the lowest possible average cost, using all of the resources available. You couldn't produce a single unit more of one thing without producing less of another. On the other hand, it is 'allocatively efficient'; the amount of utility every consumer gains when they buy the item is equal to the cost of that item to the producers. This means that exactly the right amount of effort is being put into making the product – it is a direct reflection of how much people want it. And that means the resources of a society are being shared out – or allocated – efficiently.

Even from this short description, you might have noticed the catch. Examples of a perfectly competitive market in the real world are hard to find. Some markets do come close. Outside of the realms of plant-based, lactose-free options, would you notice the difference between one pint of milk and the next? Milk is milk, isn't it? Similarly, refined sugar is essentially the same product whoever is selling it. In both cases, there are a large number of sellers and little brand loyalty, leading to healthy competition and low prices.

But in general, markets aren't perfect. There are barriers to entry; not all companies are selling products of identical quality; not every buyer and seller is a God-like, omniscient figure. You've probably already thought of half a dozen examples of imperfect markets as you've been reading. The model of perfect competition is just that – a model. And, as George Box reminds us, even the best models are wrong.

Look at the zip on your trousers or your coat. Chances are that you'll see three letters: YKK. At the turn of the 2010s, the vast majority of zips were made by Japanese company YKK. They were one of the strongest and most complete monopolies you've never heard of, providing zips for clothing, bags and almost anything else. Even with the rise of new competitors from China in recent years, YKK – a single company – still accounts for around half of all the zips made worldwide.

YKK is far from the only example that shows us how quickly our model of perfect competition disintegrates on contact with the real world. For one thing, it is clearly not true that every good has many sellers. How many businesses can you think of that produce relatively niche products like tennis racquets? For another, not all versions of the same product are identical. Even when there are multiple businesses offering similar products, they work hard to differentiate themselves from one another through branding. No true tennis connoisseur would ever confuse a Dunlop racquet with a Tecnifibre racquet, even if they're actually fairly similar (sorry, tennis fans).

This means there is often a limited number of sellers in the market. In the extreme, there is just a single seller of a good – a monopoly (*mono* being the ancient Greek for one, and *polein* being the ancient Greek for 'sell'). If there are two businesses selling something the market is a duopoly, and if there are a handful of sellers you are looking at an oligopoly.

In all of these circumstances there is 'imperfect competition' – the perfect market of countless competing sellers has eluded us. This disrupts the basic rules of how the market works. Without the threat of competition from rival businesses, monopolists (or oligopolists) no longer have to be price-takers. They can influence the market price with the decisions they make about how much to produce. The more market power they have, the more they are able to influence the price.

In the extreme – a pure monopoly with a single seller – the market price is whatever price that seller decides it should be. Even in an oligopolistic market that has just a few sellers, those businesses can get closer to the pricing outcome of a pure monopoly if they work together. This is known as collusion. As far back as Adam Smith, economists have been noting that 'People of the same trade seldom meet together, even for merriment and diversion, but the conversation ends in a conspiracy against the public, or in some contrivance to raise prices'.[3]

It's in the interest of businesses to gain this market power, because it allows them to generate more profit. In an uncompetitive market, individual businesses can produce less stuff and push up the price of the smaller number of things they do sell – after all, who is going to come in and undercut them? In turn, their profit rises above the minimal amount that you would have made if the market was competitive.

This is great news for the businesses involved, but not so good for the customer. The business's extra profits are being extracted from buyers in a way that wouldn't happen if there was more competition. If perfect competition delivers the socially optimal amount of things, the monopoly – by definition – will under-produce it. Some no longer get the product at all, even though they would be willing to buy it at a lower price that would be profitable for the producer. Those who do buy it get the same benefit as before, but they now have to pay more for it.

The result is a less-efficient economy. It contains waste – a misallocation of economic resources known as 'deadweight loss'. By capturing more of the economic benefits of production for themselves, the monopoly is reducing the overall benefit to everyone else. Thus the monopolist is better off; the world is worse off.

The downsides of monopolies are not just felt in the short term in the form of lower output and higher prices. More broadly, they can contribute to a more stagnant economy – defined by a lack of innovation and progress. If you're a monopolist, you have no fear of a competitor coming in to challenge you, so why would you need to come up with new ideas? In well-functioning markets, the threat of competition helps to keep businesses on their toes – they have to continually improve themselves or they get left behind. History shows that when a monopoly is in town this innovation can slow to a halt.

The textbook example was Microsoft and Internet Explorer. In 1999 the US Department of Justice brought charges against Microsoft for anti-competitive behaviour. It said that the company's strategy – bundling programs, particularly Internet Explorer, into its operating system and making it difficult for users to install software from competitors – was a monopolistic ploy. The allegation was that Microsoft was creating an artificial barrier to entering into the market. One of the key findings of the subsequent hearing was that Microsoft had consistently acted to deter innovation by competitors: innovations that would have benefited consumers, but that were not in the interest of Microsoft as a monopolist.

For all these reasons, monopolies are the classic example of 'market failure'. And where markets fail, policymakers tend to step in – usually through regulation and anti-monopoly, or anti-trust, policies. In the UK, the Competition and Markets Authority is tasked with policing anti-competitive behaviour. It investigates mergers between companies and steps in when a company seems to be getting too large for comfort. In the US, the Federal Trade Commission and the Department of Justice fulfil a similar role – investigating the economic role of giant companies and trying to stop any one business getting enough market power that it can abuse it.

If monopolies lead to higher prices and economic inefficiency, why are there so many of them in the world around us? You will have seen monopolies – or near-monopolies – in transport, technology and health, to name a few. Why don't we try to eradicate them completely, moving ourselves closer to the nirvana of perfect competition?

The simple reason is that there are circumstances in which a monopoly can actually be quite useful, and can lead to a better outcome for people other than the monopolist. To understand why, let's pay a visit to an ice-cream van. At one time or another, on a sunny summer's day, we've surely all considered setting ourselves up as an ice-cream seller. In some respects it is the ideal job; you bring joy to people everywhere, get to drive around all day listening to catchy music (admittedly on repeat) and you have access to as much frozen confectionery as you could want. For those brave enough to take the plunge, a second-hand, kitted-out ice-cream van can cost as much as £20,000. After that, you'd have to get registered as a business, be checked for various regulations and be trained on how to work a Mr Whippy machine. All told, the start-up cost could be around £30,000. This is known as the fixed cost, because you have to pay it regardless of how many lollies you sell. The other part of your costs is, of course, the lollies themselves – let's say at a cost of £1 each when bought from a wholesaler. These are variable costs: if you stock one ice lolly, the cost is £1; if you stock 100, the cost is £100.

Now, imagine your aim is to cover your costs. On day one you sell a single, solitary ice lolly. All of your costs have to be paid off by that one ice lolly. So you would have to charge £30,001 to scrape by. That's an expensive treat. Alternatively, let's imagine you hit the jackpot and secure a parking space on a sunny beach on a busy day. Demand from the hungry sunbathers means that you can sell 30,000 lollies. Your variable cost has gone up from £1 to £30,000, but your fixed cost remains the same. So altogether those ice lollies cost you £60,000 to supply. Per lolly that is just £2: much more reasonable.

This is an extreme (and slightly silly) example, but it shows how industries with high fixed costs lend themselves to monopolies, or at least oligopolies. A bigger business can produce stuff more cheaply, and so undercut its rivals on price without taking a hit to profits – a phenomenon known as 'economies of scale'. These large fixed costs also act as a barrier to entry – if you think £30,000 for an ice-cream van is a lot, wait until you hear how much it costs to set up a power plant or a new railway network – which automatically makes the market less competitive and violates the conditions of perfect competition.

These cases demonstrate that things aren't quite as simple as 'competition good, monopolies bad'. Economies of scale can actually be beneficial to consumers. They explain why supermarkets can sell things more cheaply than your local newsagent, or why large rail networks are often run as a monopoly with a single provider. In the United States in the 1800s, there were lots of relatively small businesses trying to provide train tracks, sometimes with competing lines just yards apart from one another. This was a source of great inefficiency. Over time, through mergers, companies going bust and government intervention, the market for railroad provision moved towards a single, more efficient monopoly, able to take advantage of economies of scale. Because of the high fixed costs of setting up a new railway, customers got a better deal if there was just one provider.

In markets with high fixed costs, lawmakers might even legislate to create *more* monopolies – because they are the only way to get businesses to produce a socially useful product. Consider patents. A patent is a legally mandated monopoly – it means that, by law, one business has the right to be the only producer and seller of something, usually for a specified amount of time. As with many monopolies, these patents can lead to underproduction and higher prices. In 2021, a study by Oxfam claimed that pharmaceutical companies Pfizer/BioNTech and Moderna were using their monopoly power – granted by legal patents – to charge as much as \$41 billion above the estimated cost of production for their Covid-19 vaccines.[4]

Why, then, would governments legislate such monopolies into existence? They have a clear economic rationale; by some estimates, the average cost of bringing a new drug to market is around \$1 billion – all spent before you've sold a single dose. If you were thinking of making such a big investment, you'd want to be relatively confident you are going to make your money back. But what if after you've invested all of that time and money in developing the new drug, somebody could come along, take your formula and make their own version? You would have to share all of your sales with them, and compete over the price. The real rub here is that, because they don't have to earn back any research costs, they can probably offer the drug cheaper than you can.

If you knew this could happen, would you invest in developing the drug in the first place? Almost certainly not. This is why pharmaceutical companies around the world are awarded patents. A patent means that, if a business undertakes a risky and innovative investment, it's likely to pay off because the patent-holder alone can sell the resulting product. Paradoxically, in these cases monopoly is driving innovation, not impeding it.

Markets with large economies of scale and fixed costs are not the only ones that tend towards – and even sometimes bring benefits from – monopolies. A natural monopoly can also form if there are huge benefits to lots of people using a single good or service. Take social media. Which social network do you use? More than likely the one that all of your friends are on. That's because a social media platform that no one else uses is not much good. In fact, the more people who use that specific platform, the more useful it becomes – you are more likely to find the people you want to connect with online.

This phenomenon is known as the 'network effect', and it is particularly pronounced in an age of giant tech platforms. Facebook currently has around 3 billion users worldwide, Twitter 400 million and Instagram 1.4 billion.[5] This means that when you join any one of these networks, chances are that some people you want to follow and communicate with will also be on there. Now, imagine a new social media site that starts with three users – you and your two authors, say. Sadly for us, it is unlikely you want to communicate with these people; you almost certainly don't know them. That means the value to you of signing up to the network is low. The result is another kind of natural monopoly: new players struggle to compete, because it's in everyone's interest to join the existing, dominant player in any given market.

It's not just social media, either. If you already have an Amazon Prime account and a Kindle, then you may well get more utility from an Alexa home assistant than from one of Amazon's competitors – because the Alexa will be more easily integrated into your network of gadgets. So dominance in one sphere – and a high degree of 'networked integration' – can lead to a natural monopoly in another.

All this means that in some cases – when there are high fixed costs, or strong network effects – monopolies are actually good for consumers. And while the lack of competition can often reduce incentives to innovate, there are cases – such as the development of drugs and medicines – where it turns out that monopolies foster innovation. In these cases, we often find that the state will keep a watchful eye over monopolies, to try to make sure that society benefits without any excessive exploitation by the monopolist. This is why industries that tend towards natural monopolies, such as train networks, energy provision and even finance, are often regulated by government watchdogs, representing a combination of state and market coming together.

All in all, however, monopolies reveal the perils of placing too much faith in markets left to their own devices. They show that, in such circumstances, markets can let us down. What's more, in some cases they show that less competition is no bad thing. And if this is true of railways and social networks, it is even more so when you start considering other markets – like education.

Prior to 1998, students going to a UK university paid no tuition fees. Zero. Obviously there were other costs – books, accommodation and so on – although even then, many students received grants that covered these expenses. Then, in November 1997, the government introduced legislation that allowed universities to charge a maximum £1,000 annual contribution from students towards their tuition. A report had highlighted the precarious finances of British universities and outlined the economic and social reasons why a larger part of that funding gap should be met by the students themselves. As it turned out, the 1997 introduction of fees was only the beginning – at least in England.6 In 2006, tuition fees at English universities rose to £3,000 a year; in 2012, they tripled to £9,000, much to the chagrin of a generation of students – many of whom took to the streets in protest.

The debate around tuition fees and who should pay for them is complex, and often fraught. But at its heart, it comes down to a core economic concept, which is particularly important if you want to understand how and why markets fail: externalities.

An externality is the side-effect of an activity on people who aren't directly involved in it. This side-effect means that the costs or benefits to society as a whole are not the same as the costs and benefits to the person involved in the activity itself.

What does this look like? Take higher education. In the case of going to university, the effects on the people actually involved are fairly straightforward. Each potential student will be thinking hard about their personal pros and cons, their private benefit and costs. On the benefit side, going to university will likely mean you earn more money over your lifetime, even though there is an initial opportunity cost of not earning a full-time wage while you're studying. If you're a bookish person, you might value a period of being surrounded by huge libraries and smart academics. If you're a social butterfly you might value the chance to join societies and sports clubs that include like-minded people. On the cost side, there are the tuition fees, as well as the time and effort given up to study.

What is less likely to feature are the costs and benefits of this decision for the wider economic and social system. For example, societies with higher rates of university-educated people tend to be more productive, more law-abiding and have higher levels of civic engagement.[7] This benefits the economy and society as a whole. This is an externality: the social cost or benefit of the action differs from its costs or benefit to the people involved.

If, as is the case with education, the social benefit is greater than the private benefit – a positive externality – then markets will tend to underprovide the good relative to what is desirable for society as a whole. Why? Because the individual deciding on how much to buy will only buy to the point that they feel their private need is met; and if the cost is too high for them personally, they may not buy at all. But this is a problem: this price won't take into account the wider benefit that their decision would have. This is a market failure: left to itself, the market is not going to provide enough of that thing, and so here too government policymakers might be inclined to intervene. Their goal: to increase the provision of that good or service to the point that is best for society as a whole.

Although few newspaper editorials put it in these terms, different ideas about externalities underpinned the tuition fee debate. If you believe that the benefit of doing a degree went pretty much exclusively to the person studying and no one else – that is, the positive externalities are small – then you may well push for relatively higher tuition fees covered by students. On the other hand, if you believe there is a large benefit to everyone in a society having low-cost access to university education and therefore encouraging a larger number of graduates – that is, the positive externalities are large – you might push for a relatively larger contribution from the state: a subsidy.

However, positive externalities are not the only kind. This is where climate change comes in. When it comes to climate change, externalities feature heavily – except this time they're far less desirable. In 1990 the cost of producing electricity by burning coal was just over 1p per kilowatt/hr. The cost of an alternative fuel source such as wind was more than fifteen times that. So is it any wonder that an energy producing company, when weighing up how to produce the electricity it needed, chose to use coal? Is it surprising that, in 1990, fossil fuels made up over 91 per cent of all energy consumed in the United Kingdom?[8]

Except we now know that this price, set by the market, didn't reflect the true cost of the two means of producing electricity. Generating energy from coal creates around twenty times more carbon emissions than wind power. This in turn has led to increasing global temperatures, erratic weather patterns and an impending climate emergency.[9] Closer to home, the cost to you of turning on your central heating for a few hours rather than putting on a jumper might not seem that much, but only because the price of your heating doesn't truly reflect the cost to the environment and the world around you.

This is the flipside of externalities. Burning coal has a big negative externality associated with it that isn't taken into account by the person producing it, or the person burning it. Just as a positive externality in education meant that it would be under-produced if left to the market, a negative externality in the form of carbon emissions means they are over-produced in a market free of intervention. This, at heart, is why markets might struggle to solve the climate crisis if left to their own devices – climate change is the ultimate negative externality.

Of course, the climate emergency is far more complicated than that, and there is far more going on than just a negative externality. In fact, the climate emergency sees a whole host of market failures colliding. Hark back to the chip dilemma in the Bank of England's canteen. As we've seen, this is a classic example of what Garrett Hardin called the Tragedy of the Commons. The common good – our collective chip supply – is undermined by the individual interests of the canteen's users – all of whom want as much delicious fried potato as they can get hold of.

You may have guessed that hungry Bank staff are not, in fact, the greatest losers in the Tragedy of the Commons. Since Hardin formulated his theory, it has been applied to any number of shared resources. Most famously, it offers a compelling example of how market failure can drive changes to both the climate and the natural world more broadly.

Consider fishermen. Why do fishing companies tend to overfish the seas, even though it will eventually deplete the very stocks they depend on? In this situation, their individual interest – to get as much fish as possible – is at odds with the collective interest – to preserve the ecosystem of the seas for future generations. Forestry poses the same dilemma: why are large parts of the rainforest cut down in an unsustainable way every year? Again, this is because the individual interest of the foresters – to harvest trees for wood in the here and now – is at odds with the collective interest – to keep the rainforest thriving in the long run.

You might think the fisherman or the logger would know that their actions would have an impact on their income and well-being in the future. Wouldn't they take that into account when deciding how much to fish now? The trouble is, the economic evidence tends to show that when people make their decisions they give significantly more weight to the here and now than they do to something that's a long way off. In almost all cases, your horizon is unlikely to include the type of multi-generational timeframe in which problems like climate change, deforestation or even long-term investment in health and infrastructure play out. Mark Carney, the former Governor of the Bank of England, termed this phenomenon the 'Tragedy of the Horizons' in the context of climate change. It is a short-termism that leads to market failures, which create issues for the future you, and for future generations.[10]

Is economics just useful in understanding this problem? Or can it offer us some solutions? Sadly, economists can't single-handedly save the world from the climate emergency. But economics can at least play its part.

The first solution that economic theory might offer is regulatory. Governments could regulate the production of certain goods, or even place a hard limit on how much they could create. For example, the amount of coal that can be mined might be limited by the state. On paper, this might work effectively. The trouble is, in the real world it is very difficult to know what the economically 'correct' amount of production is, so it is hard to know what quota to set. To do that we would have to be able to accurately calculate the precise size of the externality and its cost to society – not just now, but over the course of hundreds of years. The numbers involved would be dizzying. You would have to tot up the effects of so many interactions that any number that came out would be, at best, a finger in the wind. This is why we usually leave such large calculations to the power of the market. But in this case, the market isn't working – that's the problem.

An alternative is to try to change the costs that people encounter, to better reflect the costs to society. The easiest way to do this is through taxation. In 1920, the English economist Arthur Cecil Pigou wrote a famous book on externalities, long before the existential threat posed by climate change became apparent. He advocated a tax – now known as a Pigouvian tax – that would raise the price of goods for which there is a negative externality. Ideally the tax should raise the price to exactly cover the additional cost of the externality. For instance, if the true cost of burning fossil fuels, once the environmental cost is taken into account, is double the market price, then the tax should be 100 per cent.[11] Of course, calibrating this tax might be hard to do, but given underlying market forces, elasticities and the law of demand, it is reasonably reliable to say that making something more expensive will lead to less of it being demanded.

Pigou argued that such a tax would mean that decisions could still be left to people pursuing their own self-interest, using market mechanisms and incentive. Except now, those decisions would be priced at their true cost – and so be aligned with a socially beneficial outcome. Similarly, in the case of positive externalities, there should be a subsidy provided to lower the cost to the individual – and that subsidy should be set so that it reduced the price to reflect the social benefit. Although first outlined more than a century ago, Pigou's ideas are still hugely influential. The Pigou Club is a group of some of the most qualified economists around the world. It has been advocating for the application of Pigou's ideas to reduce the use of fossil fuels and avert a climate disaster for almost twenty years. In a different context, a Pigouvian subsidy is what those free tuition fees were trying to offer.

There's also a second solution, of a rather different kind. This is not to reduce the role of markets, but increase it. Some argue that issues of externalities arise not because markets aren't working, but because there just aren't enough of them: there are missing markets. The argument goes that if people were able to trade the true cost of fossil fuels – to buy and sell the impact of the externality – then the market would find a price that reflected that cost.

This idea was mooted as a criticism of Pigou by the economist Ronald Coase in the 1960s, and has since been developed into practical proposals for addressing issues including climate change. In 2005 the European Union set up an emissions trading scheme (ETS). Under this scheme, the EU sets a cap on how much carbon dioxide and other gases can be emitted in total. This total level of emissions is set to reduce over time, in line with the EU's climate objectives. So far, so regulatory. Where does the market come in? Within that cap, anyone wanting to produce carbon must buy their share of the total. Anyone currently holding a share of the emissions total (usually in the form of a permit) that manages to reduce their carbon dioxide emissions can sell the excess share to others who have a higher demand for it. This means there is a market-based incentive to reduce carbon emissions, and a financial cost to producing carbon. Through the standard mechanisms of supply and demand, the market for the ability to emit CO_2 will determine a price that should more accurately reflect the negative externality. The idea of a market for carbon, and more specifically for ETS-style schemes, gained traction through the 2010s. At the time of writing, there are more than thirty of these in existence, in countries ranging from New Zealand to South Korea.[12]

A final response to the potentially harmful effects of markets on the environment came from the late Nobel Prize-winning economist Elinor Ostrom. Her research focused on the commons – and the reasons they might not always be as tragic as people like Garrett Hardin had concluded. She studied communities around the world, from India to the US, Kenya to Turkey. Bringing together a range of techniques from different disciplines, Ostrom showed that when communities have control over their common resources they don't actually deplete them to destruction – in fact, they often come together in a way that ensures sustainability. Her point wasn't that Hardin was always wrong; rather that his theory only held in certain circumstances. According to Ostrom, the key is that those affected by the depletion of the resource have a voice in the decision-making.

Ostrom's work, and the economic research it has inspired, presents an alternative policy prescription to the world painted by the Tragedy of the Commons. It says that a world defined by community collaboration and empowerment – rather than intervention by the state – could prevent the Tragedy of the Commons eroding the natural world. If Ostrom's prescriptions were implemented, they might just be able to save markets from themselves.

Used-car salesmen have a reputation for crookedness. Think of Matilda's dad in the book by Roald Dahl, or Boycie from the TV show *Only Fools and Horses* – each doing whatever it takes to trick and dupe the unwitting buyer into paying more than they should.

This is perhaps unfair: aggressive negotiating and sales tactics can be found in many spheres of life, and if a salesperson was that unscrupulous then word may well spread – ultimately damaging their business. But the stereotype is rooted in an economic reality: a fundamental power imbalance between the buyer and the seller. The seller knows far more about the underlying quality of the car – how carefully it has been driven, how it performs in the cold – than the person looking to buy. As a result, the customer is at risk of walking away with a less-than-reliable auto.

This is something the Nobel Prize-winning economist George Akerlof may well have learnt the hard way, if his seminal 1970 paper 'The Market for Lemons' is anything to go by.[13] The paper explored the economics of dud second-hand cars – referred to as 'lemons'. He showed that if people are unable to accurately tell the quality of the car they are buying, they will assume it to be of average quality, and therefore only be willing to pay, roughly, an average price. This means that sellers of high-quality cars will not be willing to sell, because they can't get the price they deserve; and yet sellers of lemons will be more willing to sell because they are getting a better price than they would if everyone had the full information.

The whole process leads to a perverse situation in which there are incentives rewarding lower-quality production. Lemons proliferate; good cars diminish. The result is a feedback loop of an ever-diminishing quality of cars available for sale. This is one more way in which the model of perfect competition fails: not everyone has access to all of the information, and so in a world of 'information asymmetry', markets let us down.

Akerlof's principle can be applied in many situations. For instance, insurance companies have become adept at dealing with the lemons problem. Faced with two people and no information about them, an insurer cannot tell which is likely to be a risky driver and which a safe and cautious one. Their default would be to assume both drive with an average degree of safety, but then the reckless driver is getting a far better deal on their insurance, relative to how much risk they represent to the insurer.

To overcome this, insurers become as informed as they can about the people they are insuring. That's why there are so many questions on the forms. Some now even put a box in your car to monitor how you're driving in real time. However, even this box is an example of the 'adverse selection' that Akerlof identified. If you're a terrible driver, you have little incentive to get a monitoring box – the uncertainty works in your favour. Whereas if you are a good driver it pays to have one, so more good drivers will opt for the box. But reckless drivers beware – insurers have all read Akerlof, they know about adverse selection, so if you opt to not have the box, they might just assume you're more likely to be a bad driver and charge you a higher premium anyway.

Akerlof's insight can also be seen in the murky world of paid reviews. In 2020, Amazon deleted around 20,000 reviews of products sold on its website after the *Financial Times* alleged that some reviewers were posting thousands of 5-star reviews, apparently in exchange for payments. Some estimates concluded that almost 60 per cent of the things being sold on Amazon.co.uk were being given fake reviews to make them seem more attractive.[14]

The reason why sellers were willing to provide these sometimes large financial incentives for people to write fake reviews was because they understood the consequences of information asymmetry. They knew that buyers had less than full information about the product they were thinking of purchasing, so they would be looking for as much information as possible to balance the scales. These unscrupulous sellers were looking to exploit that informational advantage, and even solidify it further, to sell more lemons to their unsuspecting victims.

The consequences of imperfect information can also be seen in the climate debate. It is a complex and at times confusing subject.[15] Many people simply do not know what the full consequences and costs of the decisions they make are. Is it better to get an electric car to replace your old combustion engine, or does the environmental cost of producing the battery outweigh the gains of lower exhaust emissions? Without full information it is impossible to make informed decisions, and this will dramatically increase the probability of making a choice that is less than perfect.

Much like ending up with a dud car when you think you've bought a reliable little run-around, you might end up thinking you are doing the right thing to reduce your negative externalities, but in fact you are making them worse. Imperfect information could be further driving the climate crisis.

A few years ago, the staff at the Bank of England canteen made a radical decision. After years of selling chips at just one price – leading some of us Bank staff to shovel an antisocial amount onto our plates – they decided to differentiate between sizes.

At first, there was uproar. Many of us had become used to our daily all-you-can-eat chip buffet. But after the disgruntled conversations in the lunch queue subsided, the desired effect kicked in. There was less food waste – the higher prices meant people only took the chips they actually wanted to eat, and those arriving at the canteen later on were less likely to find an empty chip-pan.

The Bank of England's chip dilemma can teach us a surprising amount about climate change. It shows that markets, like all of us, are far from perfect. They fail to adequately internalise the costs of people's actions, leading to the over-consumption of finite resources – like chips. But that's not the only way in which they fail. They also lead to the underproduction of useful things, like education, and the overproduction of harmful things, like carbon dioxide. They can give rise to monopolies that act in their own interest at the expense of consumers and the wider society. And they require people to have complete information, lest they make choices that lead to them buying a dud product.

But, as the canteen staff at the Bank of England concluded, that doesn't mean that markets must be thrown out altogether. Alone, they are unlikely to solve the climate emergency, but in some ways they can help. For example, sometimes the problem might be that we just don't have the right markets. By filling in the gaps and building missing markets we can help reduce pollution, as shown by the emissions trading schemes that have been used around the world. In a similar way, Pigouvian taxes can be added to damaging activities, and so create a market-based price incentive to push them towards a socially optimal level.

Climate change is, of course, a more complex issue than central bank chip allocation. Ultimately, solving the climate emergency will take a combination of economic understanding, political will and social change. Economic theories, models and studies can only take us so far. But they undoubtedly have a role to play. And in order to play that role, it helps if everyone has a clearer sense of when markets do – and do not – operate effectively.

Chapter Three
How do I get a pay rise?

On where wages come from, frictions in the Springfield labour market, and why you should almost always consider going back to school.

In July 2019, thousands of people gathered in Arthur Ashe Stadium in New York. As home to the US Open, the stadium had played host to some of the most important tennis matches in history. But this tournament was different. The people pouring into the stadium weren't there to watch athletes, but computer geeks. They would spend the next two days encircled around computer screens, looking on as the world's best gamers played *Fortnite*.

For gaming fans, the *Fortnite* World Cup is no less prestigious or notable than the US Open. The 100 finalists in the competition had outperformed 40 million players to get to this stage. Most of the finalists played video games for a living; they had spent thousands of hours training for the finals.

Nor were these world-leading gamers merely pursuing an idle hobby. Being a professional e-sports player can be extremely lucrative – potentially more so than following other, more traditional career paths. Professional e-sports players earn around $50,000 a year being part of a gaming team, and even more if they win competitions – after which sponsorship deals from big companies usually follow. At the 2019 *Fortnite* World Cup, the victorious teenager Kyle 'Bugha' Giersdorf won $3 million; today, he earns $50,000 a month from subscribers who pay to watch him play online. Gamers who can make the leap from successful gamer to mainstream celebrity can rake in tens of millions of dollars a year.

The *Fortnite* World Cup reveals the peculiar dynamics of what economists call labour markets: the markets that determine what jobs are available, how much people will be paid for them, and whether they're able to find them. Understanding labour markets can shed light on why some people get paid so much to sit around playing video games, whilst those in other, superficially more 'worthwhile' jobs might get paid so little.

At the most basic level, wages should be determined by how much you're worth to your employer. Economists refer to this as your 'marginal product' – how much monetary value your employer makes from adding you to their workforce. The higher your productivity, or the monetary value of what you can produce in an hour, the higher your wage. A baker who can make ten cakes a day is worth more to a bakery than a baker who just makes five, and so the former should get paid more. Usually, this is key to explaining why some people get paid more than others.

Video gamers are no different. Most people play games for free, or even pay to do so, but the best get paid millions – precisely because they have a higher marginal product to their employers. There is a massive demand for the entertainment offered by professional *Fortnite* connoisseurs – as evidenced by the jam-packed Arthur Ashe stadium, numerous subscribers to online gaming platforms and sponsorship deals. When added up, the players' multi-million-dollar salaries are relatively small compared to the money made by the companies that hire them.

In comparison, if your authors were to upload a video of ourselves playing Mario Kart for an hour, we would earn very little. £0, to be precise. This is because we wouldn't generate much additional revenue for YouTube: no one would want to view videos of us going round the track. Our marginal product as gamers would be low.

At first glance, then, the world of work seems a market like any other: there are buyers (employers) and sellers (workers). However, things aren't quite so simple. Yes, labour broadly follows the laws of supply and demand. But this is also a world bedevilled with 'frictions' – which mean they cannot immediately adapt to changing levels of supply and demand. Even when there is a lot of demand for labour, the costs of labour or wages don't always rise to increase supply. In many cases, employers and employees might not even know what jobs are available: perhaps some highly skilled gamers don't even realise they could make money by playing.

This means if you want to find a better-paid job, you need to not just make sense of how markets work, but understand the peculiar ways in which they interact with the idiosyncratic economics of employment. With the right tools, you may be able to boost your pay, even if you're terrible at playing video games.

In some ways, labour markets operate much like other markets. In Chapter One we learnt how in a competitive market the price of goods is determined by the interplay of supply and demand. Labour markets are no different.

The supply of labour is the workforce – how many people are in jobs, and how many are unemployed and actively looking for work. If you're reading this during your lunch break in an office or scrolling through LinkedIn looking for job openings at home, you're part of the labour supply.

The size of this supply is determined by many factors. On a macro level, it depends on the size of the working population – in Britain this is usually defined as people aged between sixteen and sixty-four – but the size of the labour force can change over time for any number of reasons. It might change because of net migration; for example, Miami's working population increased by 7 per cent in 1980 in the wake of a mass migration of Cubans to the US, the result of a sharp economic downturn in their home country.[1] Or it might change due to cultural shifts; women are much more likely to work outside of the home now than they were in the mid-twentieth century, and that means millions more people are today part of the workforce.[2]

But being part of the labour force is also a personal decision. On a micro level, your choice to work might be determined by how much you can earn, and whether it's more than the non-work-based income you receive – welfare payments or pay-outs from shares you own, for example. Another key factor may be whether you actually enjoy working – if you hate your job, you might decide to work less, even if that means taking a pay cut. Or you might stay in a job even if you can earn more in another, because you like the culture of the organisation you work for.

Some people might not work at all. By working, you're essentially deciding to spend less time on leisure. Instead of writing this book, your authors could have spent more time reading books by a pool somewhere. After a while we would probably miss writing policy briefings. We would probably also need to earn some money to pay our bills and fund our expensive coffee habits. Meanwhile others, like retirees, might have saved up to not have to work. Some people might not work because they're students, they are looking after dependents or because they have long-term illnesses. These people are not considered unemployed: rather, they are not counted as part of the labour supply at all, because they aren't looking for work.

The picture is further complicated by the fact that nobody is permanently in or out of work, even on a day-to-day basis. People don't work all their waking hours, even if they would earn more by doing so. In fact, as people's hourly wages get higher, they tend to work fewer hours. When, in 2019, a Spanish TV reporter quit her job live on air after thinking – mistakenly, as it turned out – that she'd won the lottery jackpot, she was in fact demonstrating a powerful economic principle: that when you earn more, you often work less. Those on lower salaries need to work long hours to have a reasonable quality of life; so as you earn more, you need to work less to get by. All this means the labour supply is complicated – constantly growing and shrinking as a result of cultural norms, economic policies and the general proclivities of the workforce.

Then there's demand. This comes from employers, who have to decide how many workers they need. This time, however, things are a little more complicated. Demand for labour is unlike other forms of demand. The demand for labour is not an end in itself – people don't want your labour for its own sake. Rather, it is 'derived demand': derived from the demand for the good or service the worker is producing. Like labour supply, this ebbs and flows with time. During recessions, consumption falls and businesses might shut down or downsize, thus reducing the demand for workers. Demand for labour also depends on the availability of alternatives – your employer might be able to replace you with a robot, for example.

For all their idiosyncrasies, labour markets work like most other markets – the balance of supply and demand determines your wage. Relative imbalances in supply and demand for labour – that is, the number of people available to do jobs versus the number of people looking for workers – partly explains why your wage may go up or down. When there is a shortage of workers in a particular area – say because it requires extremely niche skills, or high levels of training, or it is simply very unpleasant – you will generally be paid more. Computer scientists are paid a lot because not enough people know how to code relative to the amount of demand for coding. Commercial deep-sea divers are paid a lot because not many people want to spend months at a time on a boat and hours at the bottom of the sea in dangerous conditions.

This is just the market's ever-present invisible hand trying to get people to take jobs that they might otherwise avoid. So the shortest answer to our question is also the simplest: grab your fins and take a job as a commercial deep-sea diver. Or another role that employers struggle to fill.

We are aware, however, that for anyone who has ever struggled to find a job this answer will be irritatingly useless. 'Find a job that is hard to fill' is easier said than done. The reason is that labour markets don't work perfectly and instantaneously. They contain frictions – forces that stop supply and demand always matching up smoothly. And so there will always be unemployment in any economy.

In the eighteenth and nineteenth centuries, early economists – sometimes called 'classical economists' – put together a rather unforgiving theory about why people were unemployed. Classical economists concluded that unemployment was simply a result of over-supply. It arose because there are more workers than there are jobs available. For example, if there is a surplus of window cleaners in an economy – more cleaners than windows to clean – wages will fall to a level at which some people won't be willing to clean windows for the wage offered. They will decide to be unemployed instead.

In this view of the world, unemployment is construed as a choice: people are deciding not to work at the wage determined by the market. Put another way, the wage that was on offer wasn't sufficiently high to entice workers out to work: the 'reservation wage' at which would-be workers saw it as worthwhile to start looking for a job was not met.

But over the next hundred years, other economists spotted some problems with this theory. It didn't hold up. First, it was criticised by John Maynard Keynes in the early twentieth century. He said that unemployment was caused by a lack of demand for things that required workers. As the twentieth century wore on, economists picked ever-larger holes in the classical theory. They increasingly recognised that labour markets often deviated from the smoothly functioning way in which they were supposed to behave. Not everyone can immediately quit their job and retrain when the economy changes; not everyone even knows what jobs are available.

That means that today economists tend not to assume people are choosing to be out of work. Rather that they are often victims of involuntary unemployment. The 'classical' theory has given way to the 'new classical' theory – one that focuses on changes in the supply of labour.

This unemployment can take several different forms. First, cyclical unemployment. As we'll explore in Chapter Nine, the economy's performance goes in cycles – with periods of great economic success and other periods of economic hardship. This has huge implications for workers. The number of jobs can change quickly in the course of an economic cycle: during boom times, businesses expand and go on hiring sprees; during recessions, they close and lay people off. The size of the labour supply changes much more slowly, though. This means that during times of economic hardship, many people are forced into unemployment.

The relationship between the jobs on offer and levels of unemployment is captured in a simple piece of economic analysis. It involves looking at the number of job adverts in the economy (the number of vacancies), and comparing it with the number of people looking for jobs (the unemployment rate) – and then comparing the two on a graph. If the concept of cyclical unemployment is correct, then during a typical downturn the number of vacancies would fall and the unemployment rate would rise. In the 1950s, the economists Christopher Dow and Leslie Arthur Dicks-Mireaux demonstrated that such cyclical unemployment was common. They named the graphical representation of this concept the 'Beveridge curve', after one of the founders of the British welfare state, William Beveridge – a man who actually had nothing to do with the curve, but presumably the authors felt would approve of their findings.

However, the notion of cyclical unemployment cannot explain all the unemployment in an economy. Economies can have lots of unfilled jobs as well as lots of people looking for jobs. For example, after the 2007–8 economic crisis, some economies had both high levels of unemployment and high numbers of job vacancies.

This leads us on to our second form of unemployment: structural unemployment. The late 2000s construction industry offers an insight into how it comes about. In the US, many construction workers found themselves out of work when the demand for houses fell, but when they looked for other jobs they discovered there weren't many that they were qualified for. There was high demand for bankruptcy lawyers at the time, but that didn't require skills like bricklaying or cement mixing. The unemployment was caused by a structural change in the economy, for which the workers available were ill-equipped. Such structural unemployment can take a long time to fix. It involves nothing short of rewiring what jobs people are able to do.

Economists have been mindful of the importance of cyclical and structural unemployment for decades, and policymakers have long attempted to reduce these types of unemployment when they come about. In recent years, however, many economists have come to focus on reducing a third form of unemployment: frictional unemployment.

Frictional unemployment relates to the fact that, regardless of how well the economy is doing, there will always be some people who are between jobs. Think about the last time you were filling in CVs and applying for jobs. There might have been a drawn-out interview process, or it might have taken you a few attempts to find the right role for you. This lag between leaving one job and finding the next means that even in an extremely efficient, booming economy, there will always be some people who are out of work. There are, in a word, 'frictions' between the people looking for a job, and the jobs themselves.

The Nobel Prize-winning economists Peter Diamond, Dale Mortensen and Christopher Pissarides have tried to make sense of the effects of this frictional unemployment.

They have developed what are known as 'search and matching' models, which explain how it can take time to match people to jobs. These models take account of the fact that people might not even know what jobs exist. In an economy the size of the UK's, between 600,000 to 1 million jobs tend to be advertised every three months.[3] How are people supposed to find them? What if some people end up stuck in the wrong jobs? And how can you know whether you should quit one job in the hope of getting another, better one? All of these frictions stop the labour market operating as smoothly as it might. They reduce what economists call 'matching efficiency'.

In recent years, new technology has gone some way to reducing these frictions – job sites like LinkedIn and Indeed mean people have a greater knowledge of what jobs are available than ever before, but frictional employment will always be with us. Regardless of how well the economy is performing, job-market frictions mean we can never have zero per cent unemployment – even if there were identical numbers of jobs and jobseekers on the market. The world of work is simply too complicated.

In the *Simpsons* episode 'Last Exit to Springfield', Mr Burns offers the workers of Springfield Nuclear Power Plant a new contract. It's the same as the old one, except instead of their free dental plan, Springfield's workers are offered a free keg of beer. At first, Springfield's workers are jubilant – free beer! – until Homer Simpson remembers that Lisa needs a new set of braces, which were previously going to come courtesy of the company. He rouses his colleagues into action, mounting a chair and tearing the contract to pieces.

Over the next few weeks, the workers of Springfield launch a bold attempt to keep hold of their existing employment benefits. Meanwhile, Mr Burns comes up with increasingly audacious ways to reduce their power over him, whether by running the plant himself or sending in hired thugs to sabotage the workers' attempts to organise. The two sides' methods offer a neat distillation of how workers' terms of employment are set – and how you can get a pay rise without looking for a completely new job.

On one level, these dynamics are simple. Workers and employers don't have identical bargaining power. They don't always need each other equally – sometimes, employers desperately need their workers; at other times, they can replace them at a moment's notice. Usually, the ease with which workers can be replaced determines whether they can realistically ask for a raise (or dental plan).

But what determines the relative ease with which workers can be replaced? At the level of whole economies, it is down to the amount of employment. The relationship between wages and employment was an obsession of the New Zealand economist William Phillips. Phillips was an eccentric and visionary fellow. In 1949, he created an analogue computer, which ran on water, that he used to model the economy: the Monetary National Income Analogue Computer (MONIAC). It passed water between various tanks at different speeds, to show how different parts of the economy respond if you change the amount of money within it.

Today, however, Phillips is best known for developing the 'Phillips Curve', which shows the relationship between unemployment and wages.[4] When unemployment is high, wage growth is low; when unemployment is low, wages increase. The basic concept is that when there aren't enough jobs to go around, workers don't have much ability to negotiate a pay rise – because there is a queue of unemployed people who would be ready and willing to come and take their jobs. This means workers don't have a lot of bargaining power. At the same time, employers aren't thinking about expanding their businesses as there isn't the demand for their products. They are going to be less receptive to calls to pay workers more.

Conversely, if the pool of unemployed people is low – for instance during an economic boom – businesses are more likely to be looking to expand, and to take on more workers. This means the pool of workers wanting jobs dwindles: employers have to offer more money to entice people into work, or to attract people who are already in other jobs. And so wages go up more quickly – the labour market is said to be 'tight', and workers have much more bargaining power.

Phillips is reported to have come up with this relationship over a weekend in the late 1950s, and it has since been placed at the heart of economic models. It is particularly important for modelling rates of inflation because, as we'll see in Chapter Six, wage rises are a major contributor to price increases across an economy. In many countries, this has been integral to policymaking for the last half a century. However, it is far from uncontroversial. Some economists doubt it exists; others believe it does exist some of the time but isn't very useful because the labour market is complicated by myriad other factors – all of which affect the relative power of workers in different ways.

For example, even if there are lots of jobs across an entire economy, that doesn't mean there are lots of jobs on offer in the area where each individual is based. Workers are not completely mobile. While the workers of Springfield could move to another town, such as neighbouring Shelbyville, they might be reluctant to do so. And within Springfield, the nuclear power plant is by far the largest employer, and so many workers can only be employed by Mr Burns' company – they operate in a 'monopsony'. This means Mr Burns thinks he can keep wages and benefits low, even if workers ask for more pay. As such, the relative mobility of labour informs the bargaining power of workers.

Or consider the use of technology. Once his workers walk out on him, Mr Burns decides to run the power plant himself, along with his assistant, Waylon Smithers. To do so, they bring in a new generation of robot workers in boxes marked '100% loyal'. Unfortunately, the robots soon take over the plant, chanting 'Crush, kill, destroy' and sending Burns and Smithers running for safety. However, not all technological innovations backfire so badly. Automation – the process through which once-human tasks are replaced by new technologies – has long been a feature of the workplace, often reducing the relative bargaining power of workers against their bosses. Although automation is not always straightforwardly bad for workers – some robots may complement the existing workforce, making them more productive and boosting wages – in the case of Springfield Nuclear Power Plant this does not seem to have been Mr Burns' intention.

Above all, however, the relative bargaining power of labour is determined by levels of organisation among workers. Homer does not take on Mr Burns alone. He has his epiphany about the perils of giving up his dental plan at a company-wide meeting, in which workers from across the power plant have come together to vote on whether to accept the new contract. After he has turned against his new terms of employment, he convinces his fellow workers – organised into a union – to work together to push for a better deal. Eventually, they go out on strike.

After several doomed attempts to break the spirits of the striking workers, Mr Burns accedes to their demands. Why did the striking workers' methods work? Because the collective bargaining power of the workers together exceeds the individual bargaining power of any one of them. By coming together, the members of the union have improved their conditions of employment. Such strikes don't always play out in workers' favour, though. William Phillips would point out that their success depends on the substitutability of the workers – that is, how easily they can be replaced. In Springfield, clearly an alternative workforce proved difficult to find, especially after the evil robots malfunctioned. But this isn't always how things work out. Sometimes the striking workers' jobs can be automated and sometimes employers can bring in other workers who are looking for work.

Whether they are successful or not, the effects of strikes can ripple out across the wider economy. Increases in the price of labour can increase the cost of the goods or services being produced. During the Springfield strike, Mr Burns retreats to a hidden room in the power plant and turns off Springfield's electricity supply. This is presented as an act of spite; however, some economists would no doubt characterise it as the inevitable result of the increased cost of producing electricity in the absence of workers, which has made Burns' business unviable. Homer's strike, in this rendering, has passed on greater costs to the people of Springfield.

In all of these cases, though, the basic rule of labour markets holds true. Workers must add 'marginal product' in order to be employed and demonstrate higher levels of marginal product to get a pay rise. Provided everyone is acting in an economically rational fashion, it must be more costly for your boss to find another suitable person for your job than give you the pay rise you want – otherwise they'll just say no.

If you find yourself unable to source enough co-workers to use your collective bargaining power, there is another way of boosting your earnings – over your lifetime, anyway. That is investing in yourself.

Here, too, the goal is to boost the marginal product of your labour. According to the American economist Gary Becker, when you invest in learning new skills, you make yourself more productive – and in turn more profitable for your employer. This could help economies become more productive and so boost economic growth. Economists refer to these skills as 'human capital'.

There are many ways to bolster your human capital. The most obvious is through formal education, by going to school, college or university. As we saw in Chapter Two, going to university boosts your lifelong earnings by hundreds of thousands of pounds – even more if you have a master's in the right subject. That's because you are qualified to do more highly skilled jobs, which generate higher monetary value. You have a higher marginal product if you are designing mobile phones than if you're loading shelves in a supermarket – and to do the former, you probably need a degree.

More education doesn't always pay off financially, though. In the UK, people with a master's degree (like one of your authors) tend to earn more than people with a PhD qualification (like the other).[5] This is because people with PhDs typically want to be university lecturers rather than investment bankers, and, relative to master's, lots of PhDs are in subjects that are less commercially focused. Likewise, not all degrees are equal. Some degrees are likely to boost your lifelong earnings more than others – for example, five years after university, medicine, economics and mathematics graduates on average earn the most, while art, agriculture and psychology graduates earn the least.[6]

But if that's put you off that PhD, there are other ways to invest in your human capital. You can acquire skills through informal means, like learning on the job – or playing video games in the evenings, as our *Fortnite* champions learnt. Most employers know that providing training for their workers helps boost how good they are at their jobs, improving productivity. Many companies provide apprenticeships to help increase skills for this reason.

Unfortunately, human capital can also depreciate in value. Imagine you're a professional athlete who is unable to work because of an injury. After a few months' rest, you might start to try to go for a light jog, but you quickly realise you're a lot less fit than you used to be. You get out of breath quicker, your muscles ache as soon as you set off and your technique is rusty. In much the same way, people who have been unemployed for a long period of time might find their human capital has decreased in value.

When this reduction in human capital is permanent, it is called 'hysteresis'. If people lose their jobs in a recession, they may become demotivated, lose out on training or forget skills they've learnt previously. Hysteresis is one of the most corrosive effects of economic downturns, because it has long-term economic (and social) consequences that can be hard to undo. For example, some studies suggest that students graduating during a recession are likely to earn less ten years after the downturn than students graduating during a boom.[7]

For all these reasons, many economists think that education is essential to building and maintaining human capital – and one of workers' and employers' main priorities should be boosting it. Many economists, but not all. There is another way of thinking about education: as a mode of sending a signal. Michael Spence, a Nobel Prize-winning economist based at New York University, doesn't think education in and of itself helps boost your marginal product or wage. In Spence's model of education and earnings, some people are innately more productive in certain fields than others. The problem for an employer is how to distinguish between the highly skilled, more-productive workers and the lower-skilled, less-productive workers.

With this in mind, Spence suggests that education sends a signal to employers as to who is high value and who isn't. In this analysis, Spence's most talented students' marks do not reflect a high level of training; they signal a pre-existing high level of intelligence. This iconoclastic theory has profound implications for education policy. It indicates that if you are innately a low-productivity worker, spending lots of money on education is a bad idea – it won't actually improve your marginal product to your employer. Nonetheless, whether it is because you are boosting your human capital or merely sending a 'signal', all economists agree that getting a good grade in a useful qualification can increase your lifetime earnings. It is perhaps the hardest, but most effective, means to secure a higher salary.

In the early 2000s, Dave Walsh left his summer job working with his father at the post office in order to play the video game *Halo*. At this point, most parents would despair. Walsh's dad did not. His son had crunched the numbers and conclusively demonstrated that his earnings from playing video games significantly exceeded those from his summer job. His father gave him his blessing.

It was the right call. At his first tournament, Dave won $5,000 – more than he would have made at the post office. Two years later, he signed a three-year contract worth $250,000 to join an e-sports team. Six years later he had made enough to retire.

Walsh's story offers a microcosm for how individuals' wages are set within labour markets. His marginal product at the post office was relatively small: franking packages adds relatively little value to the post office's turnover. His marginal product to the e-sports team – in the form of lucrative sponsorship deals and prize winnings – was much greater. Dave had made the economically rational decision: to leave the post room behind and become a gamer.

While they may not have been familiar with *Halo*, Walsh's is a story that the classical economists of the nineteenth century would have understood. According to classical economic theory your wage is determined by the supply of labour (you and your willingness to work) and the demand for labour (who is willing to employ you). If you're not happy with your level of pay, they would argue, you would leave the workforce.

However, in other respects Walsh's tale is unrepresentative. In the twentieth century, economists came to acknowledge that labour markets are a bit more complicated than the classical model implied. There have always been open jobs in the economy and people in need of jobs, but unemployment has never reached zero per cent. Just like any other market, the labour market is riddled with frictions – which stop supply and demand adjusting immediately to people's needs. These frictions mean people will always be searching for the right job, and employees for the right worker. Not everyone can just up-sticks, leave their job and train so that they can move to a more lucrative job, Dave Walsh-style. They might not even know what better-paid jobs are out there.

With these labour-market frictions in mind, the question of how to get a pay rise becomes more complicated. On the one hand, you might just ask for a raise, but this can be difficult; it depends on how much your employer values your work, or whether they can easily replace you.

A lot of workers are easily replaceable, with more workers on-hand to work for less money. But if all these workers come together to ask for more pay and threaten to leave, they might be able to raise their wage collectively.

On the other hand, then, one of the best ways of securing a high-paid and secure job is the simplest. Simple, but by no means easy. You can improve your skillset by investing in your 'human capital' – whether that's by going to university or doing more training. Education is one of the most sure-fire ways to boost your lifelong earnings. It might also ensure that you remain employable as the labour market changes, particularly if there is higher demand for more-skilled workers.

So if you want to get paid more, get yourself back in the classroom or learn on the job. Just think carefully before signing up for that PhD.

Chapter Four
Why am I richer than my great-great-grandma?

On the causes of economic growth, the promise and perils of GDP, and why the economy is more like a cake than you might think.

Imagine you have invented a time machine. Unfortunately, this time machine has very limited functionality. Instead of taking you somewhere interesting – to Londinium at the height of the Roman Empire, or Liverpool for an early Beatles gig – it has dumped you in Britain in the mid-1970s.

Your new environment is not glamorous. At every turn you see questionable fashion choices – flares, platform shoes, the odd mullet. The radio is playing T. Rex. Most restaurants seem to be serving prawn cocktail, pineapple on sticks and little else, and as you get used to your surroundings, you realise it's even more disappointing than you first thought. When you start talking to the people around you, you discover that more than half of households don't own a car, and for most people a holiday abroad is a rare treat – if it's affordable at all.[1]

You soon discover, *Back to the Future*-style, that getting back into the 2020s is harder than it seems. So you decide to settle in. As you get used to life in the 1970s, you get a job in an office, but this too proves a disappointment. It's not just the horrors of working life – a world where almost all the bosses are men, you have to write on clunky typewriters and it's perfectly acceptable for the managers to go and sink three pints every lunchtime – it's the money. Your first payslip is disconcertingly small. In 1977, the average household earned less than half of the sum earned in 2020, in today's money.[2] The country is defined by a sense of hardship: the newspapers have dubbed the UK 'the sick man of Europe', and almost a quarter of the population are living below the poverty line.[3]

So much for the 1970s, you think. But if you did manage to kick-start your time machine and go back even further, things wouldn't be any better. If you travelled to 1900, the average worker would have been earning the equivalent of £75 a week in today's money; if you went back to 1800, the sum would be £25. The further back you go, the worse off everyone becomes.[4]

In fact, life in the twenty-first century is arguably much better than in the 1970s, 1900s or 1800s. Greater wealth has led to many improvements in quality of life; higher income has led to greater life expectancy, better access to improved education and more job security. Since 1970, the average lifespan in Britain has increased by ten years.[5]

So even if you did manage to build a time machine, you may well be best off staying put, and not just to avoid the mullets.

What explains these differences in wealth and quality of life across generations? The answer is economic growth. Broadly speaking – and with some notable exceptions – your quality of life is bound up with the level of growth: whether the economy is growing, shrinking or stagnating. And the general trajectory of the economy over the last 200 years has been to increase in size.

Put simply, economic growth is the rate at which the income of the people in a country is increasing, when it is all added up. In general, when an economy is growing it can cater for increases in a country's population without lowering the standard of living. If economics is about the allocation of scarce resources, then growth creates more resources to allocate.

Growth is an abstract concept, so commentators are fond of metaphors that help to make sense of it. In the news you might see growth described as a car, variously speeding up and slowing down on a motorway; or as a garden, a rich eco-system that will only bloom if well-tended. Our preferred metaphor is a cake, which comes with less risk of petrol fumes and hay fever. In this analogy, growth makes the cake bigger – and that means there are larger slices to go around.

But how can we tell if the cake is actually growing? As we saw in Chapter One, the economy is vast – made up of millions of people and their countless choices. As such, monitoring everything that happens within an economy is a fraught task.

The US government began tackling this issue in the 1930s. It was the midst of the Great Depression, and everyone could see the economy was in trouble – with never-ending unemployment lines, countless bankruptcies and spiralling levels of homelessness. The trouble was, US policymakers had no rigorous way to measure the effects on economic growth: clearly the economy was shrinking, but it was anyone's guess by how much. That made it difficult to work out how best to respond.

To take on this problem, the US Congress brought in Simon Kuznets. An economist at the National Bureau of Economic Research (NBER), Kuznets was responsible for analysing data on the US economy. Along with his team, in 1931 Kuznets was asked to come up with a way to measure the health of the US economy. A big ask, especially in the midst of an unprecedentedly catastrophic depression. But Kuznets' team rose to the challenge. Over the next three years, they looked at different ways of adding up the economy and finally cobbled together a report called *National Income*. It developed the metric that is today used by every country in the world to measure the health of the economy: gross domestic product, or GDP.

GDP can be measured in three ways. It is the total value of everything an economy produces that can be bought and sold; the sum of everyone in the economy's income from producing those goods and services; or what everyone in an economy has spent on them within a certain period of time. In different ways, these are all measuring the same thing: the more stuff you're making and selling, and the higher its value, the bigger a country's GDP. This is captured by economists in an equation:

$$GDP = C + I + G + (X - M)$$

This equation is a rough attempt to take account of all the things that people in the economy could spend their money on. They could use it to buy things they want to consume ('C'), like a breakfast of avocado on toast. They could invest it ('I') in something like machinery. Or perhaps it could be spent by the government ('G') on the likes of roads, or the health service. There is also an inflow of money coming from people outside of the UK for the things we send them, or export ('X'), and the money going abroad on imports ('M'). When we add up all of these things, they give us the total amount of expenditure in the economy. Because the money you spend becomes someone else's income – and you must have gotten the money to spend from somewhere – this also roughly adds up to the amount produced in the economy.

It's not a perfect measure, as Kuznets was the first to admit. For one thing, he acknowledged that it fails to measure many of the things that actually improve people's lives. GDP doesn't measure happiness; it doesn't measure levels of environmental degradation; it doesn't measure inequality. And so, in many respects it doesn't measure quality of life. Although quality of life and GDP are related, there are many times when an economy is growing but the people within it might be getting unhealthier. As the US Senator Robert Kennedy once said, 'it measures everything, in short, except that which makes life worthwhile'.[6]

For another, there are many forms of economic activity that GDP doesn't measure – or at least didn't historically. Take the UK's GDP figures. In 2014, newspapers reported that GDP was about to jump by £10 billion overnight – a hike of almost 5 per cent.[7] This wasn't down to an incredibly productive afternoon by British workers, but to a change in what was included in the GDP calculation. Economists and statisticians at the Office for National Statistics decided that they should broaden the definition of 'the economy' to include more stuff. Like what? Well, prostitution, for one. And purchases of illegal drugs. In Kuznets' original version of GDP, illegal economic activity hadn't featured – but it clearly was economic activity, with producers and consumers, supply chains and businesses.

Then there are the vast swathes of legal economic activity that GDP continues to omit. Generally, the calculation ignores any activity that isn't bought or sold on the market. Consider the household labour that is essential to the functioning of society – things like cleaning clothes, doing the washing up, cooking dinner. In 2016, unpaid household work was estimated to add £1.24 trillion to the UK economy – amounting to 63 per cent of GDP at that time.[8] And yet, because unpaid housework is not part of a monetary exchange, statisticians don't count it as part of 'the economy'. This leads to some peculiar outcomes. If you vacuum your own living room, that doesn't contribute to economic growth. But say you struck a deal with your neighbour: you'd clean their living room for £20, and they'd clean your living room for £20. At the end of the day, neither of you has gained or lost any money – and your living room is as clean as if you'd vacuumed it yourself.[9] However, the very act of exchanging money means that your cleaning arrangement is magically contributing to GDP.

Finally, GDP is notoriously difficult to actually measure. When a newsreader says, 'The economy has grown by X per cent', what they really mean is: 'Economists have estimated that the amount of stuff the economy is creating has grown by X per cent.' This estimation might not be exact. Economists calculate GDP by adding up a lot of data on different aspects of the economy. In the UK, statisticians collect information from thousands of companies on topics like how many cars were made, how many houses were sold, or how much cheese was exported abroad. But this is a difficult task – there's simply too much economic activity to capture it all. So economists only ask a small proportion of the economy about their activities, and scale it up to represent the whole economy. Inevitably this figure will be slightly off, even if it's a very good guess.

Back in 1930s America, however, few politicians had time for such nit-picking. The economy was clearly tanking, and they needed a way to track it – and here was just such a method. Franklin D. Roosevelt's government would go on to use the notion of GDP to help develop economic policies during World War II, while other countries soon followed suit and adopted the measurement. Almost a century later, it remains by far the most commonly used measure for economic growth.

Why, for all its flaws, do so many governments still obsess over GDP? Because, provided you take it with a pinch of salt, GDP definitely does tell you something useful about people's quality of life.

This usually involves a bit of fiddling. Taken at face value, the GDP of France is fairly similar to that of India – but go to both countries and you'll see that France is clearly richer per person. For this reason, economists tend to use GDP per capita – that is, GDP divided between every member of the population. India has a much larger population than France, so per person it is a poorer country. The cake is a similar size in both countries, but in France each person is getting a slice that is more than twenty times bigger.

The size of this slice of cake has a huge impact on the way you live. For example, many studies have found that increases in economic growth lead to falls in poverty – one found that when GDP per capita doubles, on average the income of the bottom one-fifth of the population also doubles.[10] While this doesn't hold for every country, it's a helpful rule of thumb. Between 1981 and 2010, China lifted an astonishing 680 million people out poverty – more than the entire current population of Latin America. This was largely possible because of economic growth in the country.

More broadly, increases in GDP are associated with better health, particularly in developing countries. We know that child mortality rates are much lower in higher-income countries, as is the prevalence of diseases. In Indonesia, between 1975 and 2020, GDP per capita rose by 3.5 per cent on average a year, while in 2019 life expectancy increased from fifty-five to seventy-two years and infant mortality fell from around 100 to 20 per 1,000 live births.[11] In addition, GDP growth can pay for a better-educated population. People are more likely to go to primary and secondary school in wealthier countries, which leads to them getting higher-paying jobs in the future.

So growth matters. And fortunately enough, the long-term tendency of the global economy has been to grow – and some growth it's been, too. According to the Oxford University project *Our World in Data*, in 1500 the world economy was worth about $431 billion. In 1700 it was worth $643 billion. In 1900 it was $3.42 trillion – that's nearly eight times more. Since then, the number has exploded – reaching 10 trillion, then 50, then 100. As of 2015, the world economy was worth about $108 trillion.[12] That's a dizzying 250 times more than it was in 1500. If the cake the world was sharing in 1500 could fit into a 20 x 10-centimetre tin, the cake we were sharing in 2015 would be bigger than a table tennis table – and each person's slice is more than fifteen times bigger. We're not just richer than our ancestors: we're almost inconceivably richer. But why?

Say you set out to bake an economic cake that's big enough for everyone to have a hefty slice, with some left over. What ingredients would you need? And what recipe would you need to follow?

These are questions that many economists have asked, albeit usually without the tortured cake metaphor. The most famous answer comes from the economists Robert Solow and Trevor Swan, both of whom developed models to make sense of where growth comes from. They built on the work of pioneering economists, including Adam Smith (who we met earlier) and David Ricardo (who we'll meet shortly), to describe the four key forces driving economic growth. Economists call them factors of production:

- Land: the space on which you build your economy;
- Labour: the people producing the things that you trade;
- Capital: the machines to help the workers;
- Technology: the efficiency with which labour and capital combine.

It's easy to overstate the power of these four factors – there are an array of sociological, historical and political reasons why some economies are bigger than others. But put in its simplest terms, these four ingredients remain a useful way of thinking about your economic cake. Provided you have enough of each of these – and have got their quality and proportions right – your economy is going to rise nicely.

Why are these four ingredients so important? To answer that question, let's take a look at them one by one. First up, land. To create an economy you need somewhere to put it – just like you need a baking tin to make a cake. The more physical land you have, the more space you have for buildings like factories or offices. Of the four ingredients, this is the hardest to come by, because it is a fixed asset: once the land is all in use, it's hard to acquire more. (Although some economies have tried: in 2001, the United Arab Emirates built artificial islands off the coast of Dubai, known as the Palm Islands, on which to build new hotels and houses.)

Economists also consider natural resources – like iron ore or coal – to be part of land. Take water. It plays an important role in most manufacturing processes. In 2021, Taiwan experienced its worst drought in fifty years, putting strain on the production of semiconductors – a process that requires a large amount of water. The more water a country has, the more it can use to make things. If a country has to buy resources – import water if it's land-locked, for example – that reduces the margins on the goods and services they are producing, and so in turn this reduces the amount of GDP they could be earning.

Next comes labour. Once you have a place to build your economy, you need people to work in it – they are the bakers making your cake. The bigger the population, the more potential workers you have to make a greater number of products. It's striking that the two biggest economies are the USA and China, with populations of 329 million and 1.4 billion respectively.[13] But the number of people in a country isn't everything when it comes to labour; population demographics matter too. Labour pools with higher levels of education may have jobs that produce higher-value outputs, which in turn help the economy grow faster.

Age also matters. An ageing population can stand in the way of economic growth because older people are less likely to be in work, so they are less economically produc-tive. The most famous example of this problem comes from Japan, where nearly 30 per cent of its population are sixty-five or older, and over 86,000 Japanese are centenar-ians. Some economists have estimated that Japan's GDP will decline by over 25 per cent over the next forty years because of its demographics alone.[14] This dynamic is not limited to Japan. One study of the US population has found that a 10 per cent increase in the proportion of over-sixties decreases the growth rate of GDP per capita by 5.5 per cent.[15] An alarming statistic, considering the US population aged sixty-five or older looks set to increase by nearly 70 per cent between 2020 and 2060.[16]

Just as important are attitudes towards labour and employment. Your economy isn't going to thrive if lots of people don't or can't do any work. This is more widespread than it might sound: not because of laziness, but because of cultural barriers that discourage working-age people from getting jobs. Most notably, many women face barriers to employment, both formal and informal. In the US, around 57 per cent of the female population are employed; this figure falls to 17 per cent in countries like Algeria.[17] The cost of these gender gaps can be enormous. If, between 1970 and 2016, the growth in women's participation in the US workforce had matched that of Norway – where 76 per cent of the female population that are of working age are employed[18] – the US economy would be approximately $1.6 trillion bigger than it is today. That amounts to an extra $5,000 for every person in the country.[19]

Once you've found your land and labour, you probably need some capital. In this context, the term 'capital' generally refers to physical assets – like machinery, factories or computers. In the cake baking analogy, capital is less the flour or eggs; more the wooden spoon. Better capital may help to make more cake more quickly, or using fewer resources. You might be able to make a cake in less time using an electric whisk compared to a wooden spoon. What does that mean in a non-cake context? Imagine a clothes factory. The main types of capital that workers might use are scissors and sewing machines. Without these, the workers can't make any clothes at all. Or take an accountancy business. Accountants can't help their clients without computers to look at spreadsheets.

Sadly, capital doesn't just stand still. With time, your electric whisk might break; it might even increase the time it takes you to bake a cake. In much the same way, capital in an economy gets worn away or outdated – as factory parts break or computer software goes out of date. Without continuous improvements in capital, economic growth can stall.

That's where technology comes in. Technology might be the most important ingredient in economic growth – in fact, this was the great insight of the growth economists Robert Solow and Trevor Swan, who we met earlier. They said that technology is what multiplies the size of the cake. Although it is arguably poorly defined by economists, technology generally refers to anything that helps to improve the way we use the other factors of production. Unlike land, labour and capital, technology puts these factors of production to work. It ensures that they are combined and used in the best way possible, so you can produce more things with the same factors of production.

Think of this technology as knowledge, or 'know-how'. The more knowledge you have about making cake, the more or better cake you can make with the same baking tin (land), the same labour (you) and the same capital (wooden spoon). Technology could be a new cookbook that includes a subtly improved recipe, even if it uses the same factors of production as before.

The word 'technology' tends to conjure up images of the most dazzling and futuristic innovations of recent years: iPads, the internet, self-driving cars. But technology is so much more than this. 'Know-how' encompasses the rule of law, the invention of the wheel, and patents. Often the technologies that have most boosted growth have been fairly simple – even slightly humdrum. For example, the University of Cambridge economist Ha-Joon Chang argues that the humble washing machine has done more to drive growth than the internet.[20] Washing machines enabled people, particularly women, to spend less time doing domestic chores, freeing up time for them to enter the workforce – essentially doubling the labour supply.

Technology might be less obvious than labour, land and capital in this equation, but it's crucial. It dictates the efficiency with which the other three factors are mixed – and ultimately determines how well they can combine to produce a successful economy. That helps everyone get a bigger slice of cake without adding any more ingredients into the mixing bowl.

Once you've got to grips with these four ingredients, you can start to answer the question in our chapter title. You're richer than your ancestors because of economic growth. That economic growth comes from a combination of several factors – most notably, improvements in technology. Growth has brought with it untold benefits to your life: better healthcare, education and food; designer clothes, smartphones and plasma-screen televisions.

No wonder, then, that politicians and economists are obsessed with growth. When the economy is shrinking, it is seen as a national disaster – as anyone who watched the news during the 2007–8 financial crisis will remember. Here in Britain, achieving and sustaining economic growth is often seen as the most important economic objective of the government.

But we shouldn't get carried away. Economic growth doesn't always have a positive impact on people's lives – at least not according to some economists.

The negative implications of growth would come to intrigue the man who had pioneered its study: Simon Kuznets. In a paper of 1955, Kuznets proposed a model that outlined how, in some circumstances, growth could exacerbate inequality. The argument was simple: in the early stages of an economy's growth, income inequality was likely to follow. Kuznets argued that as economies matured, levels of inequality would ultimately fall. Nonetheless, he was one of the first economists to point out the potential problems arising from growth. Today, many economists argue that too much growth might not be a good thing. In some circumstances, they argue, growth can bring inequality, stagnating happiness and even environmental destruction.

Of these three 'bumps' in the road to a high GDP, income inequality is perhaps the most widely discussed. After Kuznets outlined his theory that growth catalyses inequality, many economists set out to test it. They found that, in many cases, he was right. The benefits of growth – and especially growth driven by technological advances – rarely fall on everyone equally.

When a new technology arrives, it disrupts the old ways of doing things. This may benefit some people, but it rarely benefits everyone – at least not in the short run. Some workers may lose their jobs, their skills rendered obsolete by the new technology. Think of the horse-and-carriage drivers who lost their jobs when cars were invented; or the taxi drivers who could imminently be forced into unemployment by self-driving cars.

A contemporary example of this process comes from supermarkets. In recent years, many supermarkets have introduced self-checkouts in place of cashiers. This benefits customers because many shoppers can check out quicker and spend less time queuing. It also benefits supermarket owners, as it's cheaper to invest in self-checkout machines than to hire cashiers. The result is greater productivity, and in turn economic growth. But there's a downside, too. Cashiers may lose their jobs, reducing their incomes. At the same time, more highly skilled supermarket workers, such as managers, might continue to keep theirs – and even ultimately get a higher share of the company's increased revenues. Overall, the shop is more productive and the economy has grown – but so too has inequality.

According to Kuznets, growing inequality is a near-inevitable consequence of rapid growth. He was particularly interested in the way inequality increases when economies start to transition from being largely agricultural to industrial – say because of advances in technology. People who already live in cities, such as factory owners, might see their incomes rise – suddenly, they can employ cheap labour from rural areas and use it to make more stuff. This increases the difference in income between those living in cities and in rural areas, as the richer people in cities get richer. At the same time, the workers in cities might also get paid very little – thanks to the influx of low-wage workers.

Kuznets believed this process wouldn't go on forever. He argued that eventually wages for lower-income workers in cities would increase. As factory owners get richer, they might increase their workers' pay; poorly paid factory workers might boost their human capital through education or skills training, and find higher-paying jobs. As the rewards of growth start to spread through an economy, our unemployed cashiers might end up getting another job; perhaps even a better-paid one.

The second bump in the road to economic growth is less widely discussed, but perhaps more important: happiness. Many economists have tried to chart the relationship between economic growth and happiness. At first, it seems, money really can buy you happiness. In the 1970s, a professor of economics at the University of Pennsylvania, Richard Easterlin, began studying data on happiness. He found that, on average, richer people are happier than poorer people; and the population of richer countries is happier than that of poorer countries. For example, within a country, only a quarter of people in the lowest income group reported they were 'very happy', whereas in the highest income group around 50 per cent of people said they were very happy.

This is hardly surprising. Rising income allows people to buy the basic goods and services that allow them to live – food, shelter, healthcare, education. So the classical theory of 'utility' that we met in Chapter One – which says that money is a good proxy for human wants and needs – seems to hold true.

But there was a catch in the data. Once a nation's wealth reaches a certain point, happiness seems to level off over time – in some cases, it actually declines. This is known as the Easterlin Paradox. For example, more recently Easterlin found that in Chile, China and South Korea, GDP per capita had doubled but overall happiness had actually fallen slightly.[21] This is true not just at the level of economies, but at the level of individuals and families. One study found that happiness rose up to a threshold of $75,000 ($90,000 in today's money) – but any further increase in salary over $75,000 did not increase happiness levels further.[22]

There's a fairly straightforward explanation for this. Easterlin said it was social comparison: people with higher incomes were only happier because they were comparing their income to people less well-off than them. But when economies grow, the less well-off earn more, reducing the gap between incomes. Meanwhile, on an individual level, as your income grows there is a 'diminishing marginal utility' on every pound you gain. In other words, for every pound you spend, you're getting a lower return on your investment in your own happiness. As we saw in Chapter One, this phenomenon holds true for businesses, where every additional pound spent tends to bring a diminishing profit. It turns out that it applies to people's moods, too. If you don't own a car, buying one could make you feel much better. Whereas if you already own three cars, buying a fourth one isn't going to make much difference to your happiness.

Then there's bump three: the environment. According to some economists, an excessive focus on growth doesn't just bring inequality and stagnating levels of happiness, it can bring destruction to the natural world. This relates to the first ingredient in our recipe for growth: land. Economic growth requires natural resources – from the oil that fuels many of our cars to the cobalt that powers our smartphones. This means that in the short term, using up natural resources can improve people's quality of life, but in the long term, the destruction of the natural world, the depletion of resources and climate change will reduce our quality of life. In this light, all the putative benefits of endless growth look short-sighted.

The fraught relationship between growth and environmental degradation isn't anything new. Take the story of Easter Island: a sparsely populated island over 2,000 miles off the coast of Chile. Today, the island is famous for its huge carved-stone statues and its remoteness. Prior to the fifteenth century, however, it was home to between 10,000 and 20,000 people: a thriving civilisation with a no-doubt thriving economy. Yet by the time Europeans arrived on the island in the 1720s, they encountered a much smaller population of somewhere around 3,000. Where had everybody gone?

The explanation, according to some researchers, is simple: the inhabitants of Easter Island had used up the natural bounty offered by the land. In the most dramatic and shocking version of this story, the problem was the *moai* – the giant stone heads that pepper the island, which were central to the islanders' religion. The story goes that the islanders chopped down the trees to make tools so that they could build and transport the *moai* around. Perhaps more likely, the islanders chopped down the trees to make the canoes they needed to go fishing. Either way, in time there were no more trees for canoes; without canoes, the islanders may have eaten other produce and animals, but without any trees, soil erosion increased and crop yields declined. The result was a catastrophic decline in population, perhaps catalysed by a civil war brought about by this food scarcity. By the time Europeans arrived in 1722, the island was almost entirely deforested.[23] Here was an example of where economic growth had led to over-exploitation of the environment.

Many anthropologists now argue that the collapse of Easter Island's population was probably a little more complicated than this story makes out. However, to many economists it still serves as a parable for the perils of excessive growth. Too much might bring environmental turmoil – but this time, it could be global. These researchers point out that most economic models omit the environment and do not take the costs of its depreciation into account. This might partly be because it's difficult to put a monetary value on natural resources. Studies estimate that in 2011 the economic value of the entire biosphere was between $125 and 145 trillion per year.[24] By comparison, global GDP at the time was $72 trillion. A recent study calls this 'natural capital' – which is visible in the quality of the air we breathe, the water we drink and the amount of green space that's available to us.[25]

The tendency of many economic models to ignore the environment seems particularly myopic because, in many cases, growth now could impede growth later. Climate change could bring untold destruction – and untold destruction tends to be bad for GDP. Some studies estimate that climate change may reduce global GDP by nearly 15 per cent by 2050.[26] We are already seeing some of the impacts of this on peoples' lives. For example, one academic study recently estimated that the 2018 California wildfires cost the US economy around £110 billion, or 0.7 per cent of the US GDP of that year.[27] And even when such a huge bill is laid at the feet of climate change, many think that attempts to quantify it can never quite do justice to the true cost of what they see as growth-induced environmental damage. After all, who can really put a price on the natural world?

You need not actually build a time machine to understand the power of GDP. If you dust off an old family photo album, you can see that we are richer now than ever before. Most of us live in better-equipped houses. Most of us go on more holidays. And most of us had better educations than our great-grandparents. This is all a result of the upward march of GDP: the sum total of how much people consume, earn and produce.

A more interesting use of your time machine might be to go forwards, not backwards. Until now, growth has usually driven greater prosperity, greater quality of life – even, some would argue, greater happiness. But this isn't always a straightforward process. Economic growth doesn't always lead to a better quality of life for everyone equally – it can result in greater inequality and joblessness. Looking ahead to the next few decades, even more striking is how much of the world's economic growth is reliant on the environment – an environment that, some would argue, such excessive growth might destroy.

This is not to say that we necessarily need to turn our back on growth. Many economies have begun to tackle climate change while also sustaining increases in GDP. Here, as ever when it comes to growth, technology is crucial. In response to the climate crisis, many economies have increased their investment in green technology. This investment might not only help tackle environmental degradation, but could also help the economy grow sustainably – particularly if it creates new jobs and investment, which in turn contribute to GDP.

Yet the debate over the link between growth and the environment remains fraught. There are no easy answers, and economics alone cannot offer all the solutions. The next time you do find yourself in a time machine, fast-forward a thousand years and see whether your descendants will, once again, be better off than you are.

Chapter Five
Why are so many of my clothes made in Asia?

On comparative advantage, the remarkable power of trade, and the great bra shortage of 2005.

Look at the labels on the clothes you're wearing now. What do you notice? Apart from finding that you might need a new T-shirt, if you're in the UK you may find that pretty much everything you're wearing has been made abroad. Nor is it just your T-shirts. In our living rooms we counted 'Made in' labels from over forty countries. Our lamp was made in Denmark, our sofa in Italy and our TV in Taiwan. Ikea is a Swedish company, but our Billy bookshelf was made in Germany.[1]

If there was enough room on the bookshelf's label it would actually say 'Made in Germany, Slovakia, Bosnia, China, Poland, Czech Republic and Romania'. The initial design was developed by a furniture designer in Sweden, the wood is from trees in Poland, and the screws that hold the shelf together are sourced from China and Poland. The manufacturing took place in Germany, using machines from another country. Then, finally, the finished book-cases were shipped to numerous Ikea warehouses around the world ready for sale. Our shelf has been produced in at least half a dozen countries, and perhaps more.

The more complex the item, the more it seems to travel. On average, a smartphone has travelled around the world nearly twenty times during its manufacture, drawing on inputs from nearly fifty countries. An aircraft wing might be shunted back and forth across borders a dozen times before it even gets attached to a plane.

While all this swapping and changing sounds dizzyingly high-tech, there's little that's new about the principle. Trade has been happening for centuries – long before the era of planes and online shopping. That's because trade offers a clear economic benefit to those who undertake it. This chapter will explain how.

The Bank of England's fastest triathlete is Jennifer Clark. In 2021, she dazzled attendees at the Europe Triathlon Championships when she swam 1.5 kilometres, cycled 40 kilometres and ran 10 kilometres in an astonishing 2 hours and 11 minutes. When she returned to Threadneedle Street the following Monday, the assorted Bank staff – not, it must be admitted, the world's most athletic bunch – were awestruck at the newfound Olympian in their midst.

Impressive stuff. But Jennifer's record pales in comparison to the record of the world's leading triathletes. At the time of writing, the record for the 'standard distance' triathlon – the length practised in the Olympics – belongs to Simon Lessing. At the 1996 Triathlon World Championships, the British triathlete completed the 51.5-kilometre course in 1 hour, 39 minutes and 50 seconds. That was 18 minutes of swimming, 50 minutes of cycling, and 31 minutes of running.[2]

Pretty fast. But not as fast as the world's fastest specialist swimmers, cyclists or runners – far from it. The record for the 1.5-kilometre swim belongs to China's Sun Yang, who completed the distance in 14 minutes and 31 seconds; the record for a 10-kilometre run belongs to the Ugandan Joshua Cheptegei, with 26 minutes and 11 seconds; and the world's fastest cyclist – Belgium's Victor Campenaerts – could complete a 40-kilometre track in about 43 minutes.[3] Even the fastest triathlete in history isn't as quick as the fastest dedicated swimmer, cyclist or runner.

The news that the central bankers aren't as fast as professional triathletes may not be particularly shocking: after all, economists are paid to develop economic policies, not to run, swim and cycle. But it hints at a crucial economic principle: the power of specialisation. Specialist, full-time triathletes are faster than non-specialist, part-time ones, and the fastest people of all are those who specialise even more – focusing on only one skill, be it running, swimming or cycling. Specialisation explains why Simon Lessing isn't as good at writing research papers as we are; but also why we aren't as fast at running as Simon Lessing. It also explains why Simon Lessing isn't as fast a swimmer as Sun Yang, a runner as Joshua Cheptegei, or a cyclist as Victor Campenaerts.

To understand the economic implications of specialisation, it's worth delving once more into the work of Adam Smith. In *The Wealth of Nations*, Smith argued that specialisation by workers benefits the entire economy, just as specialisation among athletes would speed up the overall triathlon. This specialisation, he argued, was the primary force driving increases in economic efficiency.

To make his case, Smith tells readers about a pin factory he had visited. Writing at a time when industrial machinery was just beginning to transform the landscape, Smith was dazzled by the efficiency of the mills and factories popping up across Britain. The value of these factories, Smith argued, was that they allowed greater specialisation – the 'division of labour' between different workers.

In practice, Smith observed, each worker focused on one element of the pin-making process. Making a pin involved about eighteen different tasks: drawing out the wire, cutting it into pieces, putting on the head and so on. If the factory's staff of ten people each did all eighteen tasks themselves, they would barely manage to make two pins each a day. But if each person specialised in a particular element of the pin-making process – I chop up the wire, you put on the head, and so on – then the same ten people could produce more than 48,000 pins a day. As Smith wrote, 'in this manner, divided into about eighteen distinct operations, which, in some manufactories, are all performed by distinct hands'.[4]

The benefits of specialisation were manifold, Smith argued. It meant workers didn't need to waste time switching tasks – not just moving to each new workstation but also getting into the swing of each new role. It also reduced the time and resources required to train each employee: factory owners only need to teach each worker one task each, instead of all eighteen. This saves both time and money, leaving factory owners with bigger profit margins – and, perhaps, allowing for higher wages for the workers themselves.

What's more, doing the same task repeatedly also means you become better at it. You might even become an expert. Pin workers who focused on just putting on the pin heads might have become more skilled at it than others who focused on chopping up the wire. What's more, some pin-factory workers might have been naturally better at one part of the production process than others because they had better eyesight or greater dexterity – and so were better suited to fiddly tasks than tasks that involved brute force. Overall, if each worker just did the task they were better at than any of the other workers in the factory, it would result in better-quality pins all around.

Almost 250 years later, this insight into the importance of specialisation remains one of the most powerful ideas in economics. So powerful, in fact, that the old £20 Bank of England note depicts Smith's famous pin factory on its back, along with a not-so-catchy quote: 'The division of labour in pin manufacturing: (and the great increase in the quantity of work that results).'

This quotation made it onto your cash because its implications go far beyond just pin-making. Consider our triathletes. The same principles explain why it's quicker to have specialist runners, cyclists and swimmers than just a single triathlete. Triathletes have to change outfits and shoes for each leg of the race, from their wetsuits to their cycling Lycra to their running shoes . Even Olympic athletes take between 30 and 45 seconds to change kit.[5] If there were three different athletes taking part in the race, it would shave 75 seconds off race times – and also save some unfortunate changing mishaps.

What's more, it would free up each athlete to focus on getting better at the task in which they have an advantage – running, swimming or cycling. Day in, day out, they could practise their running technique, for example. If each of the world's fastest specialist athletes focused on their own preferred part of the race in a relay, they would reduce the time of the overall triathlon by 15 minutes and 12 seconds. Specialising in something narrow wouldn't just benefit the individual athlete; the whole team would complete the race quicker.

In economic terms, specialisation tells us that it's better for everyone to stick to what they're good at – and let others do what they're good at, too. It's true in a pin factory, where specialisation leads to a dramatic increase in productivity. It's true in a triathlon, where specialisation means everyone finishes the race sooner. Moreover, it's true in every sphere of economic life – within the Bank of England, economists and security guards are different people, each playing to their relative strengths. Economic degrees don't come in handy when trying to guard bars of gold from potential burglars; in turn, a nous for disarming intruders isn't that useful in developing economic policies.

Since Smith's time, the full power of specialisation has been unleashed to an extent that he could barely have imagined. Many factories only produce one tiny aspect of what goes into a final product. For example, there are factories that make only one of the many microchips in your phone, or just one small part of a car which is then assembled elsewhere. These parts don't have very much value in themselves – but when they combine with other specialist parts, they make up the objects on which we all depend.

What does pin production have to do with your T-shirt? Well, specialisation and division of labour also applies at the level of whole countries.

Imagine a world in which every nation had to produce its own goods at home. Bank of England economists would have to eat shepherd's pie and Yorkshire pudding every day, using only produce farmed in the UK. We would all be wearing tweed. This book would have been written on an old-school Imperial typewriter, without American software to check for spelling mistakes. It would be incomprehensible – even more so than this version.

We're exaggerating, of course. But the principle holds. Thankfully, this is not the world we inhabit. Just like Smith's workers in the pin factory, countries tend to specialise in producing certain things – the things they're best at making –then swap these items through trade. Taiwan is known for its microchips; Germany is known for its cars; France is known for its wine. Here in Britain, we produce a lot of financial services. Why? Because British companies are good at it.

These national specialities can develop for any number of reasons. For example, the UK is good at providing financial services because it has a highly educated workforce and a strong legal system. As the financial sector has grown in the UK, more and more people have trained to join it, further enhancing Britain's specialisation in the area. As people become better trained and specialised, they can provide better financial services at a cheaper price than countries that have fewer people working in the sector.

Sometimes, these specialities develop thanks to local geography. For example, Cremona in Italy is well-known for making violins. It all began in the sixteenth century, in response to the increased demand for instruments for royal families. Two essential types of violin wood – maple and spruce – were readily available in the Lombardy region, and so Cremona was a natural hub for this nascent industry. This sector then took on its own momentum. Over time, many craftsmen in the city specialised in making bowed instruments. To this day, Cremona produces 80 per cent of the bow stringed instruments that are exported from Italy each year.[6]

In other words, every country can have an 'absolute advantage' in producing certain goods or services – whether thanks to the climate, or history or luck. In many cases, other countries can't hope to compete with the nation that has such an absolute advantage. One country or region is better at making something than any other, or can produce more of it given the same amount of resources. There's a reason why Britain doesn't have many banana farms; in absolute terms, Britain's climate is worse at growing bananas than Ecuador's.

But we live in an age of global warming: what if, because of climate change, the UK's climate was transformed? Imagine a world where the southern coast of England has become a tropical paradise, with Brighton's seafront dotted with palm trees and Margate beginning to look more like Miami. Would it still be cheaper to import bananas from Ecuador, rather than just grow them at home?

This is where things get more complicated – because the answer is probably still 'Yes'. Why? Because land is scarce in the UK, especially the limited land on the south coast. Even if Britain could produce high-quality bananas, making the leap to producing them would mean the UK's producers had to produce less of other things – such as strawberries, potatoes or wheat.

This is what economists call comparative advantage. It's doing what you do relatively well, while giving up on what you do less well. Or, more technically, producing the thing with the lowest opportunity cost compared to any other country. Say growing a bunch of bananas and a punnet of strawberries requires the same amount of space on the UK's southern coast. It costs the UK £1 to grow a bunch of bananas but only 50p to grow a punnet of strawberries; Ecuador, on the other hand, can grow a bunch of bananas for 10p, whereas it costs 40p to grow a punnet of strawberries.

Ecuador clearly has an absolute advantage in fruit farming. It can produce both fruits at a cheaper cost than the UK. But by growing both fruits, Ecuadorian farmers are giving up the chance to grow four times more bananas for every punnet of strawberries they plant, the fruit which costs them the least to grow. Similarly, it costs British farmers twice as much to grow bananas as to grow strawberries on the UK's southern coast. This means it's more profitable and less resource-intensive for British farmers to focus on their punnets and Ecuadorian farmers to focus on bananas. It would be economically beneficial for the UK to stick to strawberries, Ecuador to bananas, and for the two to trade these fruits with each other. Both countries are better off as result.

The theory of comparative advantage was one of the great theoretical innovations of the nineteenth-century economist David Ricardo, who we met briefly in the last chapter. Born half a century after Adam Smith, Ricardo was a wealthy businessman who discovered economics after reading *The Wealth of Nations*. Ricardo took Smith's theory of specialisation and applied it to whole countries – arguing that an economy boosts its economic growth by focusing on the industry in which it has the greatest comparative advantage.

But Ricardo was also clear that for comparative advantage to bring its full benefits, it required something else: trade. Countries need to exchange goods and services, with countries focusing on those in which they have a comparative advantage. Trade means that, even though Britain grows strawberries, Italy designs violins and Taiwan makes microchips, you can buy strawberries, violins and microchips in London, Milan and Taipei.

Trade was nothing new, even in Ricardo's day. The Silk Road, one of the oldest trading routes in the world, linked China and the Roman Empire from the second century BCE onwards.[7] But slowly and surely, through history the amount of international trade has grown. By the seventeenth century, you could buy potatoes, tomatoes, coffee and chocolate in Europe, even though these were products of the Americas. The invention of steamships and trains in the nineteenth century then took global trade to hitherto unimaginable levels. As Keynes observed in 1919, 'The inhabitant of London could order by telephone, sipping his morning tea in bed, the various products of the whole Earth, in such quantity as he might see fit, and reasonably expect their early delivery upon his doorstep.'[8]

Fast-forward to the twenty-first century and we live in a world of trade that even Keynes – writing over a century ago – could barely have imagined. Over the last century, the heady cocktail of specialisation and cheap transportation have led to more global exchange than ever. In fact, trade has increased by more than 4,000 per cent since 1900.[9] This is one reason why the world feels like a smaller place. Globalisation – the growing interdependence of the world's economies – means that the vast majority of goods and services consumed around the world have been sourced from multiple countries.

Here, then, is the answer to why the T-shirts in your wardrobe are made in Asia. Asia's greatest comparative advantage is its low labour costs. China, where many of our T-shirts are made, has a mainly low-skilled and large population, so wages are low. The average worker in China in 2019 was paid 90,501 yuan a year – about $14,000. In America, meanwhile, the average salary was $53,490 in 2019.[10] There are fewer people in the US and, on average, they are more highly educated and so they demand higher wages. As such, it is cheaper for tasks that involve lots of unskilled labour – like making T-shirts – to take place in developing economies, such as China. The Chinese economy's focus on manufacturing has helped to bring cheap goods to most countries, and turned the country into an economic powerhouse – with over 128 million manufacturing jobs, which contribute to nearly a third of the country's GDP.

As the economy has become even more globalised, what gets traded between countries has shifted. Physical goods remain important: according to the World Trade Organization or WTO, physical goods made up 77 per cent of global trade in 2020.[11] But the scale of trade means the production of these goods becomes more specialised than ever. Most physical goods now require inputs from many different countries. In 2020, Apple was reportedly sourcing parts from nearly thirty countries – each making a highly specialised different part of its products like iPhones.[12]

But trade is not limited to physical stuff. The transfer of services now makes up 23 per cent of global trade. These services are often based on the exchange of ideas such as research and development; they rely less on labour and more on technology such as the internet. This transformation is tangible in the way we consume music and film. When was the last time you bought a CD to listen to music or a DVD to watch a movie? We can't remember either. The shift from physical goods to digital services such as streaming and subscription services can be thought of as a different kind of trade – one in which information and data, rather than any physical product, is being exchanged. Although not officially counted in most trade statistics, this digital exchange is vast: including flows of digital information such as email, YouTube content and social media. Such trade adds up to $8.3 trillion in value annually – a figure that would amount to an increase of overall trade flows by 20 per cent if included in official statistics.[13]

*

Does this mean that more trade is always an unambiguously good thing? Some people think so – leading inexorably to cheaper, better goods, and jobs in the places that are best suited to them. But many argue it's not quite so simple.

Over the last twenty years, the alleged problems arising from free trade have become a political hot potato. Across the developed world, starting in the late twentieth century, rich countries that once had large manufacturing sectors had seen them decline. These sectors found themselves unable to compete with the low labour costs of countries in Asia and other parts of the developing world – leading manufacturing jobs to be 'offshored' to lower-income countries. If we were writing this in the mid-twentieth century, there would have been a good chance that our T-shirts had been made in Britain; these days not so much.

Understandably, the decline of manufacturing jobs in higher-income countries has proved controversial. In the most extreme cases, it has led countries to introduce policies that protect their domestic industries and workers from foreign competition.

Cast your mind back to summer 2005. Prince William graduated from the University of St Andrews, 'Crazy Frog' was storming the charts, and the PlayStation Portable (PSP) had just landed in shops across Europe. We, your authors, were unassuming teenagers with only the most nascent interest in global supply chain logistics; in fact, our main interest was what to wear to the beach. But whenever we visited the shops, we found the clothing rails empty. What was going on?

The explanation: a trade war. The term refers to an escalation of barriers to trade between countries. Even in an age of globalisation, trade between nations is rarely completely 'free'. Many countries impose tariffs, which are essentially taxes on imports brought from abroad; or quotas, which limit how much one country can export to another. In a trade war, countries impose more or higher barriers against rival countries. These wars don't involve tanks or infantry – they might be more aptly called trade spats – but they can still cause great disruption.

In the case of the 2005 incident, the warring (or spatting) parties were the EU and China. There had long been a worldwide quota on all textiles known as the Multi Fibre Agreement (later called the Agreement on Textiles and Clothing), which limited how many clothes could be exported from developing countries, like China, to developed countries, like those in the EU. The agreement protected clothes makers in developed countries from losing market share to countries in which clothing could be produced a lot more cheaply.

But at the beginning of 2005, the Agreement was abolished. This allowed quota-free trade in clothes. The trouble was, many countries in the western world weren't ready for the amount of competition to which they were about to be exposed. By that summer, the US had seen a 100 per cent increase in clothing imports from China; the EU an increase of over 200 per cent.[14] This was a problem. Many countries in the EU, including Spain and Italy, had long-established domestic manufacturing industries, but they were suddenly being exposed to unprecedented competition.

As a result, the EU imposed annual quotas for trade, limiting the amount of some Chinese goods that could be imported. But the Chinese government, deeming this unfair, retaliated forcefully. The Chinese flooded – or 'dumped' – more than their quota's worth of clothes into Europe within a few months. Because this dumping exceeded the numbers in their quota, the EU refused to allow many clothes into the shops – stranding some 80 million items in ports.

The row was soon named the Bra War, given the 4 million bras that were stuck in container ships or languishing in warehouses at European ports in the summer of 2005. But bras were not the only victim: so too were 48 million jumpers and 17 million pairs of trousers.[15]

So who won the war, if anyone? Customers wanting to buy a new summer outfit for their holidays fared poorly: they were limited to buying clothes from countries that did not have an advantage in making them, so they had to pay more. They also faced shortages of jumpers, trousers, lingerie – and, as we discovered on our summer holidays, swimsuits.

People making clothes in the EU benefited for a while, as Europeans now had no choice but to buy clothes from nearby countries. But many European retailers complained they could not obtain products for sale, and not at the same prices as before. And clothes makers in China lost out as they were no longer permitted to sell in Europe.

No one really won out from the trade war in the long run, then. And this is true of most trade wars. The US–China trade war that began in 2018 harmed not just the two countries directly involved, but the whole world. At the time, it was expected to lower US and China's GDP by nearly 2 per cent, and global GDP by around 1 per cent.[16]

Fortunately, in the case of the Bra War, the EU and China eventually found a compromise. The EU released the clothes and allowed China to count some of the excess as part of the following year's quota. In recent years, EU states have increased investment in high-value-added production and technology to make things such as wind turbines and electric vehicles – instead of clothes, which rely on workers. In other words, they have focused on their comparative advantage. This has kept further trade wars on clothing at bay.

However, it is impossible to remove the risk of trade wars altogether – as long as there are states with competing interests, they remain a possibility. Policymakers have tried, though. One of the ways in which countries can reduce the risk of trade wars is through trade agreements – either a bilateral agreement between two states, or a 'trade bloc' made up of several countries that pledge to abide by a shared set of trading rules. In many cases, they choose to reduce or eliminate tariffs when trading with one another, and they often negotiate a shared set of standards on goods, too. Trade wars are unlikely to happen between countries that have agreed to a common trading protocol.

Trade blocs are nothing new. One of the oldest blocs, established in 1834, was the Zollverein (German customs union) which contained most of the German Confederation – consisting of states that now make up parts of Germany, Austria, the Czech Republic, Luxembourg and other surrounding nations. Like many modern-day trade blocs, it eliminated trade barriers between member countries. Before the bloc was set up, it is estimated that there were around 1,800 customs barriers operating within the Confederation.[17] Eliminating these barriers led to faster, smoother trade – and so greater profits for traders, and better prices for costumers.

Nowadays trade blocs play a similar role. But, in a more globalised world, they are even more widespread. Within the European Union, the cost of shipping goods across borders is essentially zero. Other trade blocs you might have heard of include the North American Free Trade Agreement (NAFTA) between the USA, Canada and Mexico – now known as the United States-Mexico-Canada Agreement (USMCA). In November 2020, the largest ever trade agreement was signed when the Regional Comprehensive Economic Partnership (RCEP) brought together an existing economic union, the Association of South-East Asian Nations (ASEAN), with states including China, Japan, South Korea, Australia and New Zealand. In 2019, these countries involved made up nearly 30 per cent of worldwide GDP.[18]

These trade blocs and agreements have been one of the engines of globalisation. By lowering the cost of global exchange, they make it even more likely that your wardrobe will be filled with clothes made overseas.

In 2020, China exported just under a third of the world's clothes. Bangladesh and Vietnam exported around 6 per cent each; followed by Turkey and India. Looking only at clothes you could be forgiven for thinking that these countries were the most productive and affluent in the world.[19]

Until, that is, you change focus. Looking instead at cross-border services – a category that includes legal advice being supplied to overseas customers via email and tourists eating in a restaurant while on holiday abroad – the picture is transformed. The US is miles ahead of everyone else, exporting 14 per cent of the world's services. Next come the UK and Germany. China – the mightiest clothes exporter on Earth – comes in fifth, behind France, with under 5 per cent of the world's exports.[20]

By now, you will understand why Asia is such a superpower in clothes but a relatively meagre player in the world of services. It's a phenomenon that follows the same logic as Adam Smith's pin factory. Then, as now, the route to efficiency was specialisation.

Because this principle applies not just to factories, but to entire nations, different countries have different areas of 'comparative advantage'. In many cases, this is down to the resources available to them – it explains why Switzerland is known for its watches, Belgium for its beer and Cuba for its cigars. In other cases, though, a nation's comparative advantage is a social phenomenon: China has a knack for exporting T-shirts because of its low labour costs; the UK has a knack for exporting professional services because of its highly specialised skilled workforce.

And yet one of the greatest rules of economic history is that countries' comparative advantage rarely stays still. It would be a mistake to look at Asia's leading role in clothes production and conclude the continent is nothing more than a global source of cheap labour. Over the last few years, Asia has also become the world's primary producer of mobile phones, computers and solar panels. In a couple more decades, Asia may be the world's leading exporter of cars, too. When it comes to balances of global trade, nothing is ever fixed – the world's current largest producers may one day be importing clothes from countries that today barely make a thing.

Chapter Six
Why aren't Freddos 10p any more?

On inflation and where it comes from, why everything getting cheaper might not be as fun as it sounds, and bad Covid-era haircuts.

Up and down the United Kingdom, people are asking a burning question. It unites every British citizen – rich and poor, young and old, northern and southern. And with each year, it's a question that gets asked with greater outrage.

The question is this: What's going on with Freddo prices?

Many readers will remember the days, just a few decades ago, when a Freddo – Cadbury's iconic frog-shaped chocolate bar – cost a mere 10p. But in the years since, the grinning face of the nation's favourite anthropomorphised frog[1] has come to seem less jubilant, more mocking. By 2010, the price of a Freddo had hit 17p. In 2017 Freddo found himself on sale for an eye-watering 30p, and, even following a slight respite in 2021, at the time of writing our favourite chocolate amphibian costs a cool 25p.[2]

This book is not advocating an insurrection against Cadbury's. We realise that the rising price of Freddo has less to do with this specific product and more to do with a near-inevitable economic process – one that causes prices across the economy to gradually drift upwards. It is a process that erodes the value of money over time, reducing the amount you can buy with it.

This process is inflation. In many cases it can go unnoticed day-to-day, but over time it can seriously affect how far your money goes. In extreme situations, inflation can have catastrophic consequences; in less extreme situations, it can have a corrosive effect on people's chocolate-buying habits, as Freddo and his legions of fans have discovered the hard way.

Every year, economists and statisticians create a hypothetical shopping list that represents what the average person buys. It includes physical goods: bread, milk, shampoo; T-shirts, dumbbells, laundry powder. And also some services: gym membership, window cleaners. All this gets compiled into a not-quite-exhaustive summary of what your average household is shopping for.

Statisticians then track the cost of that shop over time and see how much it is changing – in many cases they literally go to the shops and check the prices every month. If this representative shopping list cost £100 a year ago and now costs £102, then the price has gone up by £2, or 2 per cent. That means inflation is 2 per cent.

Not everything in the shopping basket will have necessarily gone up by exactly 2 per cent. Some items may have gone up by a lot, some by a little. Some may even have become cheaper. At the time of writing, average prices in the UK have gone up cumulatively by around 20 per cent since 2010. However, the cost of coach fares has risen almost 95 per cent, a packet of peanuts has increased almost 70 per cent and the cost of going to historic monuments has increased more than 60 per cent. That trip to the Tower of London has become a lot more expensive than you would expect if you had been following the main inflation rate – especially if you wanted a snack while you were there. On the other hand, the price of men's football boots has fallen by around 20 per cent, computer game prices by almost 30 per cent, and laptop computers by more than half. So you can play football online or in real life much more cheaply than in 2010.[3]

What goes into the hypothetical shopping basket is a much-discussed question. It can depend on what you are trying to capture. If you want to know how much prices have gone up for the companies that make things, then you might look at a shopping basket of materials that go into production. Your basket would be very different if you wanted to capture what was going on with the cost of living for the average family. Their shopping basket would be likely to contain a lot more bread and milk and a lot less iron ore.

The most commonly used and discussed metric of inflation is designed to measure what are known as consumer prices. The aim is to get a view on what your average household is spending on things it consumes, and the basket is chosen to reflect that. In the UK, the task of picking this basket falls to the Office for National Statistics (ONS); similar bodies are tasked with the role elsewhere around the world.

'Consumes' is a crucial word here. House prices don't feature directly in most headline measures of consumer price inflation, but when you think about what a consumer price basket is trying to capture, that makes sense. You don't 'consume' a house – it isn't part of your regular monthly or weekly shop, used and then gone. In the UK, one of the headline consumer shopping baskets used to calculate inflation does actually make an allowance for the regular cost of housing – that is, rental costs that also stand in for mortgage payments. There are also alternative indices that capture a wider concept – the 'cost of living' – which adapt their shopping baskets to suit.

What goes into the consumption basket varies from country to country. The French list contains frogs' legs and *escargot*; Germany's contains bratwurst and schnitzel; the British list includes 'oven-ready joints', the centre-piece of a traditional Sunday lunch.[4] It also varies through time. In 1947, when the ONS first selected a basket of goods it contained gramophone records and cod liver oil. Fast-forward seventy-five years and these have been dropped and replaced by things more relevant to what the modern consumer spends their money on – Netflix, flavoured milk, condoms.[5] In 2021, in response to the coronavirus pandemic, the ONS added hand sanitiser for the first time as it rapidly became a core part of people's regular shop.

By its nature, the basket of shopping that is used is representative. Although it matches the average person, it is extremely unlikely to match what any one person actually spends their money on. So the rate of inflation won't perfectly describe the changes in your personal cost of living. For instance, the price of transport tends to rise by more than the price of eating out in cafes and restaurants. If you're someone who spends a higher proportion of their income on travel then your personal inflation rate would be likely to be more than someone who spends a larger fraction dining out.

Evidence from surveys suggests people tend to feel like the official measures of inflation under-report the cost of living increases that they face.[6] This might be because their shopping basket differs from the representative one used by statisticians. Alternatively, it may be that people tend to give too much weight to bad news (higher inflation) and not enough to good news (lower inflation). There is also a well-documented bias in which people put a higher psychological weight on prices they see regularly, such as groceries, which tend to exhibit higher rates of inflation than other parts of the shopping basket.

If you want to know your own personal rate of inflation, there are online tools that can help you calculate it. But you can also easily calculate a very rudimentary version yourself. Just keep your receipt the next time you go to the supermarket and highlight the items that you buy regularly. Then put it in a drawer and forget about it for a year. In twelve months' time, collect another receipt and find the same items. If you tot up how the price of these items has changed over the year as a percentage, then – voilà! – you've found your personal inflation rate.

Of course, if it were that easy there wouldn't be armies of statisticians around the world crunching the inflation numbers. Even in our personal shopping list example, you'll notice that there are a few complications. What if you buy more bread now than you did a year ago? Statistical authorities are always recalibrating the relative weightings of the different things in the basket to try to keep up with our changing habits.

There's also the problem of quality. How do you make sure you avoid apples and oranges comparisons? Or, to be precise, Apple iPhone with Nokia 3310 comparisons? A phone now and a phone in five years' time are hardly comparable. When it launched in 2000, a Nokia 3310 cost £129.99. The iPhone 12, launched in 2020, cost at least £579.[7] The implied inflation of almost 450 per cent doesn't tell the whole story, though. The latest iPhone can do immensely more than the old Nokia – offering not just texts and calls, but also a camera, speakers, Candy Crush and access to all the world's information via the web. So it is important that the people who calculate inflation adjust their estimations accordingly. This quality adjustment issue is most obvious in technology, where in many cases the prices for genuinely equivalent products have been falling dramatically for decades, if an equivalent even exists. On a quality-adjusted basis, the prices of goods in the UK are more or less what they were in 1988.

Even if you're checking prices regularly, inflation can be hard to see. In 2017, the UK's Office for National Statistics published a report identifying 206 products in the basket of goods that had reduced in size without seeing an equivalent reduction in price. Where you had previously got twelve fish fingers in a pack, there were now only ten. Where a box used to contain eighty teabags, it now only contained seventy-five. Most worryingly of all, if you were expecting that toilet roll to still have 221 sheets on it, you'd be shocked to find it now only had 200. Economists call this shrinkflation, and from an economic point of view it is identical to putting up prices – you're paying the same amount, but getting less stuff, so the price per unit has gone up. This doesn't always work out for the companies in question, however. When the snack company Mondelēz tried to reduce the size of their Toblerone bars in 2016, they sparked a furious backlash from chocolate connoisseurs – only to revert to the original shape a year and a half later. Even Freddo hasn't escaped shrinkflation. In 2020, Australian consumers were left hopping mad as packs of Freddos were reduced in weight and size with no change in price.

In November 1994, the United Kingdom was in the grip of a new sensation. The National Lottery offered everyone in the country the chance to become a millionaire, all for the cost of a £1 ticket. Never mind that the odds suggested your chance of winning was roughly one in 14 million. The first draw saw over 15 million people buy over 35 million tickets – all in the hope of being 'the one'.[8]

In fact, in that very first draw, there were seven 'ones', who shared a jackpot of £5,874,778. This meant they took around £840,000 each. In 1994 this was a decent chunk of money. It could buy you almost 5,000 Game Boys, a fleet of forty newly launched Toyota Rav4s, and still have change for a pair of those fluorescent rave glasses that were inexplicably popular. Or even 8.5 million Freddos. However, let's imagine that our lottery-winning raver had put their prize in a (rather large) suitcase under their bed and brought it out in 2022.[9] They might have been disappointed. Not only would they struggle to find someone to sell them industrial quantities of Game Boys, the value of their money would have more or less halved.

Since 1994, the National Lottery has given rise to a number of spin-offs and variants. One iteration – Set for Life – offers those who pay their money the opportunity to win £10,000 a month, every month, for the next thirty years. On 28 December 2020, twenty-one-year-old James Evans was probably looking forward to the end of what had been a tough year defined by the global Covid-19 pandemic. Little did he know that before the year was out he would have won the Set for Life jackpot and begun receiving £10,000 a month. He will continue to do so until he is in his fifties. One of James' first reactions was to plan a family ski trip to Canada. At current prices, fulfilling that dream would probably set him back around a month of lottery winnings. However, by the time James reaches the end of his thirty-year windfall, the same trip would likely take him twice as long to pay for, or he'd have to leave his least-favoured half of the family at home – £10,000 in 2051 just isn't going to go as far.

Lotteries are not just a modern phenomenon. They have a long heritage, with state lotteries recorded at least as far back as ancient Greece and Rome. The first national lottery in England came in 1567, created as a way for Queen

Elizabeth I to raise money without resorting to an unpopular tax rise (some might say not much has changed, there). A maximum of 400,000 tickets were there to be bought at 10 shillings a pop. The first prize was £5,000 – with some bonus prizes including plates, tapestries and, naturally, immunity from prosecution. In those days, £5,000 could buy you 1,000 horses, 4,000 cows or 1.2 million quarts of good beer. But by 1994, £5,000 would seem like loose change to the first winners of the revamped National Lottery. It would be just two weeks' winnings for James Evans in 2021. In fact, if you were looking for the equivalent spending power that £5,000 gave you in the 1560s in today's money, you would need to have won £2.7 million.

Although we might not all be lucky enough to be millionaire lottery winners, the examples above illustrate the power that inflation wields over all of us. As prices rise, the spending power of the money in your pocket falls. Over the last thirty years, inflation in the United Kingdom, and most other advanced economies around the word, has averaged around 2 per cent. This is a relatively modest amount, but even that is enough to erode roughly half of the spending power of your cash over three decades.

All this means that the rate of inflation is an emotive and highly political issue. Unless you're actively offsetting the impact of inflation, it has the potential to eat away at your spending power. For example, looking at pay packets alone, you might think that wages for UK workers had gone up by more than 20 per cent in the decade or so leading up to 2021, at a rate of over 2 per cent a year. A pretty consistent pay rise, at first glance. But once you take account of inflation, you quickly realise that the amount people could buy with that money had barely increased. Any increase in their spending power was eroded, because inflation matched the wage increases. In contrast, wage increases in Japan have averaged less than 1 per cent for more than a decade now. But over that period inflation averaged more or less zero. That meant workers were still better off in terms of what they could buy. A lower pay rise on paper, but a better outcome in terms of what matters.

In all these ways and more, inflation defines our lives. Its rate has implications for a whole host of long-term decisions – be it saving for a pension, taking out a mortgage, or even working out how much of a pay rise you can get away with asking for. That's why your Freddo is so much more expensive these days; the sad truth is that most things you buy are, too.

If you bought a daily newspaper in Zimbabwe in 2008, the headlines would have been dominated by one story: the rate of inflation. It was really high. So high, in fact, that if you bought the same paper the next day the headline may well have been the same, but the cost of the newspaper would likely have doubled. In 24 hours. The inflation rate in Zimbabwe at that time was almost 80 *billion* per cent. And if that wasn't bad enough, imagine it happening the next day – then the next day, and the next, and the next. Zimbabweans were experiencing what for most people would be a lifetime of price increases in the space of a single weekend.

Zimbabwe is far from the only country to have gone through periods of uncomfortably high inflation. From the mid-1960s to the early 1980s, the United States, and much of the rest of the world, experienced a period known as 'The Great Inflation'. A combination of oil price spikes, increased spending by governments and policies by central banks meant that prices were increasing at double-digit rates every year – inflation was regularly in newspaper headlines and a prominent feature of political debate. At those rates the price level would double, and the value of your money halve, every five to seven years. If it had kept up for thirty years, your spending power would have fallen to just 2 per cent of what it had been at the start.

Of course, 80 billion per cent is a different ballpark to inflation in the low double digits. What we saw in Zimbabwe, a phenomenon where price increases accelerate and take on a life of their own, is known as 'hyperinflation'. There is no hard-and-fast definition as to when inflation tips into hyper-drive, but if you're seeing your weekly shop go up by triple-digits year-on-year, then you can probably safely assume you're seeing hyperinflation.[10] Such hyperinflations are a recurrent force in world history. Most people are at least vaguely familiar with the hyperinflation that crippled the German economy in the 1920s, and which contributed to the political upheaval that resulted in the Second World War. You may have heard the stories of people running around with wheelbarrows full of cash trying to spend it before it became worthless. More recently there have been periods of hyperinflation in Hungary, Greece, Argentina, Venezuela and Lebanon. By some estimates, there has been an instance of hyperinflation somewhere in the world on average every two years for the last century.

Although extreme, these episodes highlight the corrosive economic effects of too much inflation. For a start, high inflation makes it near impossible to operate a business. Take a practical question like price noticeboards. In a situation of low or no inflation, you only have to change the prices infrequently, but with high inflation, you have to do this on a daily, if not hourly, basis. This comes with a cost – new signs, your time – which can add up to a substantial outlay. Even with relatively stable price increases these so-called 'menu costs' can be significant. One study on the US supermarket industry found them to be equal to as much as one-third of the profit margins of the companies involved.[11]

For those of us who don't run businesses, high inflation can have a deleterious effect on our relationship with money. Inflation reduces the value of the money in your pocket – so when inflation is high, people tend to carry less money with them, choosing instead to invest it somewhere that will give them a better return. They only take out money when they need it. This means they will tend to hold less money than is ideal, but also that they have to take more trips to the bank to withdraw money – that is, to convert the wealth they have in assets back into money. Such costs are known as 'shoe leather costs' – the idea being that you are literally wearing out your shoes by walking to the bank and back.

Then there are the costs to the government of having to keep reprinting money. When the value of money is falling so fast, even a high-denomination banknote loses its value quickly and becomes worthless. In mid-2008 Zimbabwe was running out of paper on which to print new money and couldn't afford to buy more as the paper cost more than the notes were worth. Prices were increasing so quickly, and new denominations being announced so rapidly, that there wasn't the time or capability to buy new paper with the correct watermark. In fact, prices were moving so fast that old watermarks ended up being reused. If you look at a 2008 $25 billion note, the watermark shows that at the time of manufacturing, that paper had been intended as a $500 bill. By January 2009 the highest-denomination note in Zimbabwe was $100 trillion, and astonishingly, that wouldn't even get you a bus ticket.

However, all these day-to-day problems for individual businesses, consumers and governments pale into insignificance when compared to the implications of high inflation across the whole economy. Perhaps the most corrosive impact of inflation is on how people think about their savings.

Inflation can be thought of as a tax on keeping money. Just as income tax might take away a fraction of your salary every month, inflation takes away a fraction of your spending power. At the same time, inflation reduces the value of debts. Imagine you borrowed £100 from your grandma and promised her you would pay her back £110 in twelve months' time – so she's charging you 10 per cent interest.[12] You both expect inflation to be 10 per cent that year, so the money you pay back can buy exactly the same amount then as the £100 could have before. But what if inflation were actually 20 per cent? Well, you still owe £110, but the cost of that in terms of things you have to give up in the economy is now less. Your spending power has increased. Poor Grandma, on the other hand, now has £110 but can buy 10 per cent less with it than she expected. Her spending power has fallen. All this happens because most of our debts are calculated in what economists call 'nominal terms'. Your debt to Grandma – or a bank – would be for a number, say £100, plus any fees Granny or the banker saw fit to add. It wouldn't be in 'real terms' – whatever £100 is the equivalent to at the point you have to pay it back.

This dynamic, through which inflation erodes the value of debt, has myriad effects across the economy. It leads to what has long been one of the great temptations of debt-laden governments – to deliberately bring about inflation and so reduce the burden of their debt. The catch is that this simultaneously reduces the value of the money in people's bank accounts. The debt reductions are being paid for by the inflation tax – a tax on your spending power. For the same reason, inflation tends to shift spending power away from people who have saved, and towards people who have borrowed. And because we are more likely to be a borrower when we are young and hold more assets when we are old, that usually means it shifts spending power from the old to the young.

If high inflation is so costly, why have it at all? Wouldn't it be great if the prices of things went down over time, so everything was cheaper?

This argument makes perfect sense if you think of yourself as someone who simply buys things, completely detached from anything else. The trouble is, most of us aren't just consumers: we play many roles in the economy simultaneously. We are business owners and employees, manufacturers and sellers. When you begin to think about prices going down in the context of all those different roles, you start to see why it can be just as bad as rapidly rising prices, if not worse.

Consider the story of the US at the turn of the 1930s. Following the Wall Street Crash in 1929, the United States went into a period of depression, and with it deflation. By 1932, prices were falling at a rate of 10 per cent a year. The issue was a lack of demand. People had lost a lot of money, so had less to spend. Those who did have money had become cautious after being burned by the Crash, so they held on to their money rather than spending it. All of this meant less demand for the things that businesses were selling. Businesses' response was to cut back costs and reduce the amount they were making, in the hope that they could save some of their precipitously declining profits.

The knock-on effect of these cuts was disastrous. It meant workers went home with lower wages, or no wages at all. The unemployment rate in the Great Depression capped out at over 25 per cent. Crucially, those workers now receiving lower or no pay were also customers, either for your business, or a business next door. So by cutting their income the American economy entered a cycle that lowered demand further, leading businesses to make further cuts, and so on.

Once deflation sets in, it takes on its own momentum. If you know that something will be 10 per cent cheaper tomorrow then it makes sense to delay buying it and make the saving if you can. This is particularly true for big-ticket items that you don't buy very often – think TVs, fridges and cars. When this kind of consumer behaviour is a short-term phenomenon – like when people wait for the Boxing Day sales – it's not a big problem. The issue with persistent deflation is that it always pays to delay your spending to tomorrow. And, as with the cuts in wages, the decision to delay leads to a reduction in demand today – which means that prices fall further and faster, and it makes even more sense to delay, as your savings later will be even bigger. Economists call this self-reinforcing process a 'deflationary spiral'. Once an economy is in such a spiral, it's notoriously difficult to drag it out.

Deflation also poses a troubling problem for anyone who holds debts. As we've seen, while inflation reduces the spending power of money, it also reduces the cost of debts in terms of the money needed to finance them. As £100 becomes worth less, that £100 loan you took out two years ago is less of an issue. Deflation means the opposite. The real cost of your debt goes up because now £100 is a bigger deal, relative to the cost of living, and probably your wages, than it was yesterday. This means deflation isn't quite as appealing as it might sound. Given the costs of both high inflation and of falling prices, economists almost universally agree now that the best thing to aim for is low and stable price increases. Prices should go up by a number high enough that the risk of them falling when something bad happens is low, but not by so much that they risk spiralling into hyperinflation. The exact level to aim for is up for discussion. Many high-income countries aim for 2 per cent a year; some economists make arguments for slightly higher, say 3 or 4 per cent. But almost everyone agrees that the costs of inflation become particularly severe once it has hit around 10 per cent, and the risk of it taking off from there grows rapidly.

In early 2020, many people went for what turned out to be their last professional haircut for some time. With the arrival of Covid-19, barbers the world over shut their doors. As lockdown wore on, and the global population developed increasingly bedraggled bobs, many began fantasising about the first professional haircut they'd get once the world reopened: one that came not from a housemate wielding inexpertly held clippers, but from a professional hairdresser.

But when those longed-for hairdressers reopened in Britain in the middle of 2020, customers were in for a shock. In light of the new health risks, hairdressers up and down the country had to buy new safety equipment, clean down all of their equipment more thoroughly between appointments, and spread out customers more. That limited the number of customers they could fit in the same space. And all of this increased the cost of producing each haircut. Many barbers passed that cost on: in the eighteen months following the first Covid-19 lockdown, the price of a haircut rose more than 8 per cent.

As unusual as this situation was, it offered a glimpse into why inflation comes about. At the most basic level, inflation results from the individual decisions of millions of people, day in, day out, on what to charge for the things they sell. When making those decisions, most business owners probably don't think about deep economic processes or theories. Instead, they think about what is going on with the costs they face, and how much demand there is out there for what they are selling. If their costs are higher, their prices will be as well. If they realise demand is on the up, that might tempt them to raise their prices too.

Economists tend to split the drivers of inflation along similar lines. On the one hand, there are forces – like Covid-related safety equipment – that push up prices by increasing the costs of inputs: cost-push inflation. On the other, there are forces that pull up prices by increasing the demand for products and services: demand-pull inflation.

Let's take these forces in turn. There are four major drivers of cost-push inflation. First, rises in the price of commodities – such as oil, gas or steel. Consider the price of oil. In October 1973, OPEC – a group of oil-exporting countries, mostly from the Middle East – announced an embargo against a group of western countries. They were retaliating against these countries' alleged support for Israel in the Arab–Israeli war of that year. What they didn't realise was that their decision would mark a turning point in world history. Over the next five months, the price of oil would rise by a factor of three – contributing to the wave of inflation that would define the 1970s.

This was because the implications of OPEC's decision weren't limited to oil. Oil was (and is) used somewhere in the production process of almost everything – whether as an energy source, a raw material used in the manufacture of products like plastic, or as the fuel that transports goods around the world. A rise in oil prices meant a rise in the price of everything else. Producers had two options: they could keep their prices the same and absorb the higher cost out of their profit, or they could pass on the extra cost, keeping their profits roughly the same, but increasing the price faced by the eventual buyer. If they chose the first then they would take a hit to their profits, and maybe even make losses. If they chose the second option they would be likely to see a fall in the demand for their products as the higher prices discouraged buyers. In practice they tended to opt for a mixture of the two, with consumer prices rising by over 14 per cent around the world in 1974.[13]

Movements in the exchange rate are the second major driver of rising costs. Imagine you're taking a trip to the Swiss Alps. Soon after you hop off the plane you buy a bar of Swiss chocolate. It costs 10 Swiss francs – equivalent to about £8. A bit pricey, but then you are on holiday. After a week of mountain air, melted cheese and yodelling you return to the same airport and decide to buy the same bar of chocolate. You pay the same price, 10 Swiss francs. But unbeknownst to you, the last week has seen swings in currency markets: the Swiss franc has decreased in value by 10 per cent compared to the pound. So in terms of pounds, that chocolate bar now costs you a mere £7.20. A good time to pick up another bar for yourself, perhaps. In fact, exactly this happened to one of your authors in September 2011, when the franc depreciated almost 10 per cent in a single day during their holiday in Switzerland.

Through this process, changes to exchange rates have a big impact on inflation. They can increase the cost of importing goods. In that week in 2011, Swiss chocolate makers importing milk from Germany found the prices they were paying were instantly 10 per cent higher when paid in francs. In a world in which we all depend on wood from Canada, technological parts from South Korea and coffee from Ecuador, the cumulative costs of these exchange-rate fluctuations can be significant.

Next up, cost-push inflation can be driven by increases in wages. Crucially, though, not all wage increases are equal. *Why* wages are moving, matters. If workers are getting a pay rise because they are getting better at what they do – and their productivity is improving – this may not lead to any inflation. Let's say your job is to make 100 widgets an hour, for which you get paid £10 – this means the wage bill to your employer per widget is 10p. But after inventing some new-fangled widget-making trick, you realise you can make 110 widgets an hour, and so your employer rewards you by putting your wage up to £11 per hour. The cost per widget is still 10p – so there's no cost to pass on to consumers. On the other hand, if your wage bill has increased because a company can't find the workers it needs, and so is having to pay more, that will hit the company's bottom line – and it may result in price increases.

The final driver of cost-push inflation is taxation. Consider an example from 2018, when the UK government introduced a new tax on sugar. This created a dilemma for Coca-Cola. Unlike some brands, which chose to reformulate their products to contain less sugar, the company stuck to their guns and kept to the original recipe. But that meant raising the price of a can of Coke. A similar but more widespread pattern was seen in January 2011 when the headline rate of value-added tax (VAT) went up from 17.5 per cent to 20 per cent. This means that with no other changes, the cost of a T-shirt that had once cost £25 now cost an extra 50p. This could be seen directly in the numbers for inflation, which jumped from around 3.5 per cent in December 2010 to over 5 per cent by September 2011. Economists estimated that without the VAT rise, inflation would have increased by nowhere near as much, to around 4 per cent.

Yet these 'push' factors are only half of the picture. Demand-pull inflation is anything that causes demand for things to increase by more than the economy's ability to increase their supply. That increase in demand could be driven by a wide range of factors. It could be as simple as people feeling more confident and wanting to spend more – what John Maynard Keynes called 'animal spirits', the impulsive swings in public mood that he thought drove consumer behaviour. But whatever causes the underlying increase in demand, when it outstrips the increase in supply then consumers will push up prices – as they clamour to secure goods for themselves. People are willing to pay more to get the stuff they want.

Perhaps the most famous example of a demand-pull factor that leads to inflation is an increase in the supply of money. In fact, Keynes' great intellectual counterpart, Milton Friedman, went as far as to say that inflation was 'always and everywhere a monetary phenomenon'.[14] He meant that without an increase in the amount of money circulating in the economy, relative to the amount of stuff the economy was producing, the prices of goods would never increase – at least, not in a persistent way. He had the evidence to boot. In the 1950s and 1960s, Friedman and his colleague, Anna Schwartz, undertook a statistical analysis that showed that, with reliable regularity, as the supply of money in an economy increased, so did inflation. Likewise, as the growth of the money supply slowed, prices grew more slowly or even fell.

This insight came to underpin a theory known as monetarism. Monetarism is rooted in a relatively uncontroversial idea: that ultimately the amount of money being spent must equal the value of the things being produced, imported and bought. That value is a combination of the number of things produced and their price. In many senses this is just adding up, and Friedman immortalised that process in an equation known as the Quantity Theory of Money.

From this starting point, monetarists argue that the number of things produced in the economy is – at least in the long run – pinned down by a few fundamental, slow-moving forces, like the size of the working-age population or the sophistication of technology. As such, the amount of money in circulation cannot affect the real size of the economy. This principle is known as the 'long-run neutrality of money'.

In practice, this means that you can increase the amount of money in circulation, but that won't increase the amount of actual economic activity going on. The inevitable result according to monetarists? Inflation. Each pound in circulation is diluted in value – the same amount of stuff is being bought and sold, but there are more pounds with which to do so.

In the 1970s and 1980s, monetarism became an increasingly influential school of thought in most western economies. It was the economic ideology of politicians including Margaret Thatcher in the UK and Ronald Reagan in the United States – and it led the policymakers with their fingers on the money supply (more on them later) to focus intently on the quantity of money in the system. Friedman himself advocated a fixed rate of growth for the amount of money in the economy, arguing that this would lead to a constant and stable rate of inflation.

The monetarists' conclusions stood in stark contrast to those of a previous generation of policymakers, who largely had subscribed to Keynes' view of the world. As we will learn in Chapter Ten, Keynesians had a far more hands-on approach to economic management – and tended to advocate government spending as the means of stabilising the economy, rather than controlling the money supply. In some ways, however, these two bitterly opposed tribes had much in common. Both accepted that, in the short run, the economy doesn't immediately adjust to the amount of money in circulation via inflation, and so for a time, it is possible to alter people's desire to work and how much they spend by creating money. The difference was that monetarists would argue these effects wear off fast enough to not really matter – before you know it, everything has fed into higher inflation. Keynesians, on the other hand, argued that the period of adjustment is drawn out enough to give the economy a helpful push. Perhaps inflation would follow in the long run, but then, as Keynes himself put it, 'in the long run we are all dead'.[15]

The economic tug-o'-war between monetarists and Keynesians would carry on through the late twentieth century, and it continues to this day. But by the early 1990s, the general consensus had tipped away from the purely monetarist position. This was largely because the empirical relationship between the quantity of money and output and inflation, so elegantly proven by Friedman and Schwartz a few decades previously, started to break down. Suddenly, more money didn't necessarily mean more inflation.

It was a striking change, caused by an array of economic shifts across the developed world. One was the series of seismic changes in the banking and financial sectors in the 1980s; another was the fact that policymakers began focusing on money itself, which likely changed the reliability of the connection between money and inflation – a phenomenon known as Goodhart's Law. But perhaps most interestingly of all, there was a transformation in how people actually spent their money. Even if the amount of money in the system remains the same, the speed with which it changes hands – the 'velocity of money' – can fluctuate significantly. When the same pound is being spent by ten different people in a week, then more stuff has been bought than if the same pound was used only once. A fundamental part of how monetarists viewed the world was an assumption this velocity was relatively stable, or at least predictable. You only got paid monthly, you only went to the shops once a week, and so your money was passed around at a pretty reliable speed. However, a body of evidence since the 1980s has shown that velocity can change a lot – and those changes can be difficult to foresee. That added a wholly new, hard-to-predict element to the equation. It meant that there was no simple, reliable link between the amount of money circulating and the rate of inflation.

Since the 1990s, the debate about the causes of inflation has moved on again – this time to an observation by

René Descartes: 'I think, therefore I am.'[16] The great philosopher was talking about the philosophy of existence, but his sentiment could be applied, less loftily, to one of the most fundamental drivers of inflation – what economists refer to as inflation expectations. The theory goes that what we think will happen to inflation is one of the big determinants of what actually does happen. Inflation can be a self-fulfilling prophecy.

To see why, imagine you are negotiating your next pay rise. If you believe inflation will be high, you will ask for a larger pay increase, to make sure your spending power doesn't lose pace. This means that wages go up by more. But as we've seen, the very fact of rising wages can create more inflation. By thinking high, you've pushed up the rate of inflation. Conversely, if you believed that inflation would have been low, then you would have negotiated a lower pay rise – and so across the economy inflation would have been lower. The same effect can be seen in financial markets as people negotiated contracts to lend and borrow, based on their expectation of inflation.

The importance of expectations in determining what actually happens to prices has been demonstrated time and time again. For that reason, economists whose job it is to keep inflation low and stable – like those of us at the Bank of England – spend a lot of time studying not just what people in the economy are doing, but what they are thinking. It is also why most nations have an explicit target for inflation. If you believe policymakers are good at keeping inflation at a healthy level – and the data suggests we are – then people know what inflation is likely to be.

And oddly, by believing they know what inflation is going to be, they keep it at that level.

All of this hints at a different way of thinking about your Freddo prices. Perhaps it makes you look at the increasingly pricey grinning frog with a little less anger, and a little more understanding.

You might even realise that some of the Freddo price rise is for the good, because a little inflation guards against a cycle of falling prices. It encourages people to spend today rather than hold off until tomorrow, supporting economic growth, and if you are a debtor it reduces what you owe over time. This is not to say that super-fast rises in Freddo prices would be OK, though. If prices started to double, or triple, in the course of a single year, and with them the prices of other products on the shelves, the effects could be disastrous – making it near impossible for businesses to keep running and consumers to save money.

It also matters what is causing those Freddo price hikes. Is it down to a push – a rise in the price of cocoa; or a pull – a rise in demand for chocolate treats? In some situations, the rise of Freddo prices comes from growing costs hitting businesses, forcing them to put up their prices and pushing up the general price level. In others, inflation comes from increases in demand, leading to price rises when supply can't keep up. This distinction matters: if you want to keep inflation at a healthy level, you need to know what is causing it – in many cases, some combination of the two factors.

But the most fraught debate around inflation relates less to whether it is good or bad and more to its relationship with money. For decades, the dispute about the extent to which the money supply is driving inflation has raged on. One reason, perhaps, is that money is hard to get your head around. It's another area that economists are still trying to make sense of – even 5,000 years after the first monetary system. It is this confusing but fascinating world of money that we will explore next.

Chapter Seven
What actually *is* money?

On what makes money money, why you can't print your own currency, and how you too could get the sort code 10-00-00.

What do you think of when you think of money? A debit card, a banknote, your mobile phone?

What about teeth? Chocolate? Dried fish? At one time or another all of these things have been used as currency. What is the common thread that makes each of these seemingly random objects money?

The history of money is complex. It has developed in different ways at different times and in different places throughout human history, so trying to tease out the underlying logic is no easy task. Keynes described the period of his life where he studied the origins of money as his 'Babylonian madness', because he became so obsessed with the coinage of ancient Middle Eastern civilisations.

According to some definitions, money has been around for almost as long as civilisation. Around 5,000 years ago, in ancient Mesopotamia, systems of debt developed around grain storage. Workers would keep their grain in temples or warehouses known as grain banks. A ledger – basically a spreadsheet carved into a stone tablet – was kept that made a note of how much grain you owned. You could then lend that grain or exchange it with someone else, without having to go through the hassle of taking the grain to where they were and giving it to them. The ledger became a way of keeping score of the debts that everyone owed each other. If this feels familiar, it should. The same basic premise – keeping a record of balances and transfers – underpins our modern system of bank accounts. In this origin story, money developed as a form of memory: a way of keeping score of who owed what to whom.

Precious metals have also been used as a way of paying for things for millennia. The ancient Egyptians used gold bars of certain weights in their exchanges. In Bronze Age Britain, gold was often used in ornate jewellery, which some people believe was used as a form of payment. But there is a cost to swapping metals in their unstructured form – how do you know how much it is worth? To be sure, you need to be able to weigh your lump of gold or silver and be certain that it is what it says it is. Not very handy if you're just popping down to the shops. The solution to this problem? Coins. The innovation of casting your precious metal into a certain size and shape and then stamping it with something official so people knew it could be trusted dates back to the ancient Lydians, who came up with the idea around 700 BCE. In the British Museum you can find a coin, created by King Croesus of Lydia, in the sixth century BCE – and stamped with a lion and a bull. The first paper money developed more than a millennium later, in China.

Yet money need not take such a narrow range of forms. Take the Rai Stones of Yap. These were huge stones that the inhabitants of the Pacific island of Yap had to travel across a dangerous stretch of water to mine. They then had to make the perilous journey back to Yap, bringing the stone with them. A stone's value was not based just on its size, but also on how costly it had been to obtain in terms of lives lost. It would be particularly lucky – and hence valuable – if no lives at all were lost in getting it. Similar to the grain banks of ancient Mesopotamia, the Yaps' system eventually evolved to one of keeping score of who the owner of the stone was, without having to move the stones themselves. Some stones even fell into the water on the voyage but retained their value at the bottom of the sea, because islanders knew and recorded who the owners were. This pattern of valuable but cumbersome commodities being replaced by a much more efficient and easily carried form of money is repeated time and again throughout history.

All this indicates that money, in one form or another, has popped up almost whenever there has been a group of humans who have needed to interact with each other. And thanks to the sheer diversity of human history, that means some truly bizarre objects have been used as money over the years. Prisoners of war have developed systems based on cigarettes as a form of money. Mackerel became a form of money in some American prisons in the early 2000s. In medieval Russia, squirrel pelts were a common form of money – so common, in fact, that snouts, claws and ears were also used as change. You could be forgiven for wondering what on earth all these things have in common. What is it that actually makes something money?

For something so fundamental, it is surprising that there is no universally agreed definition for money. But most economists would say that for something to be good money, it must be able to fulfil three functions, first laid out by Adam Smith – him again – almost 250 years ago.

The first function is the most obvious. For something to be money, you must be able to pay for things with it. Economists call this the 'medium of exchange' function. It means that you can give money in exchange for something that isn't money, and that someone else will accept the money because they can use it to pay for things themselves in the future – and not because they want to consume it themselves. This is distinct from, say, barter, which is when you give someone something they want to consume in exchange for something you want to consume. Barter is when I swap my chicken for your grain, so I can use the grain in my bread; money is when I swap my chicken for a rock, then give that rock to someone else in exchange for some grain.

The second function is that money must be able to carry value from now into the future, a time machine for your spending power. You need to know that if you take money from someone today, you can be confident of what it will buy you when you come to spend it tomorrow. This is called the 'store of value' function. Imagine if we used bananas as money. You could get paid ten bananas this week and be confident that if you spent them tomorrow they would have a similar value. But what if you were trying to save up your bananas to pay for a summer holiday in six months' time? Your waiter on the Costa del Sol might not be willing to accept what was left of your savings in exchange for a sangria on the beach. Bananas wouldn't hold their value. This hasn't stopped food being used as money at different points in history – it is just usually foods that last a bit longer. Salt was used in much of the ancient world, bricks of tea were used in parts of China up until the Second World War, and even as recently as 2009, huge wheels of Parmesan cheese could be used as a deposit for a loan in parts of Italy.

This longevity of value is partly what makes money so useful. It helps solve one of the fundamental problems of economic life, which economists call the 'double coincidence of wants'. Without money of some form, you have to find someone who wants what you have, at exactly the same time as you have something that they want. Even in tiny societies this is extremely unlikely. While you might enjoy reading witty and informative books on the economy, strangely, they aren't for everyone – if the local petrol station manager doesn't want a copy, it would be hard for us to fill up the car's tank by paying with books. Money solves this problem. We can exchange what we produce for money then hold on to it until we have something we want to buy; whoever we are buying from will accept it, whether they want what we produced originally or not.

The last function of money is a way of keeping score. Economists call this the 'unit of account' function, and it means that the prices of all the other things in the economy can be, and usually are, written in terms of money. How much value does that banana have? £1. What about that car? £5,000. We know the value of both cars and bananas in pounds. Having a single unit that does this is a remarkable time-saver. Without it, you would need to know the price of everything in terms of every other thing. This is what would happen in a barter economy, where there is no money and goods are just swapped for one another. It might not be a problem in a simple world where one person makes bread, one brews beer and one sells meat: in that case, to trade you would merely need to know how many pints of beer equalled one loaf of bread, how much meat equalled one pint of beer and how much meat equalled a loaf of bread – three prices. Unfortunately, this approach doesn't scale very well. An average supermarket has around 150,000 things to buy in it. Without money you would need to know roughly 11 billion prices to be able to compare things to one another. A price for eggs in terms of milk, milk in terms of bread and bread in terms of eggs, and so on. With money, this collapses down to just 150,000 prices: one for each thing.

These three functions of money are not completely separate. It is unlikely that people will accept something as payment if they don't know if it will keep its value in the future, so it is hard for something to become the medium of exchange if it is a bad store of value. Conversely, if you're not sure if people will accept something as payment tomorrow, then it becomes a poor way to store your spending power. And if people are all using one thing to pay with, it makes sense to use that to set your prices – so the prevalent medium of exchange usually becomes the dominant unit of account.

At the same time, however, these three functions don't quite get to the heart of what money is. At its core, money is trust. Money works because we all agree, as a society, that it has value. You will work hard all day and accept money because you know that the local shopkeeper will accept it. They will accept it because they know someone else will accept it when the time comes. It works because we believe it works.

In 2021, the pioneering computer scientist Alan Turing became the latest face to be added to UK banknotes. He joined a list of some of the most notable figures in British history: from Winston Churchill to Jane Austen, Florence Nightingale to our friend Adam Smith. But although the faces have changed over the years, since 1694 all UK bank-notes have included one consistent, crucial phrase: 'I promise to pay the bearer on demand ...'.

What does this promise actually mean? For much of the last 300 years it was a promise to pay the value of the note in gold. You could turn up to the Bank of England and demand your gold. This system, of money representing a claim on an underlying asset, is known as commodity or representative money. The underlying commodity could be anything: until surprisingly recently there was a cocoa standard in South America in which goods had prices fixed in terms of cocoa beans. Often societies have settled on precious metals, such as gold or silver, because they are hard-wearing – so a durable store of value – and noted for their beauty.

However, there is not much inherent in gold that gives it value, other than the fact that people tend to value it. If a zombie apocalypse came, would you rather have some food, a big steel machete or a gold bar? Gold gets much of its value in our present system because people believe it is valuable – a phenomenon that the Tudor statesman Thomas More satirised in his magnum opus, *Utopia*, which described a world where people have realised gold isn't particularly useful and so use it to make their toilet pans. When it comes to money, the uselessness of gold doesn't matter – provided people continue to believe in its value.

The system whereby you could convert your currency to gold was known as the Gold Standard. In the 1800s, the UK and many of its colonies agreed that they would exchange currency for gold at a specified rate. By the end of the century, this had spread to many more countries around the world, each fixing their own exchange rate to gold. This system meant that the currency was effectively backed by gold – and that economies had to hold enough gold to be able to fulfil demand for their currency, limiting the extent to which they could create more money.

Most parts of the world suspended the Gold Standard in the First World War, only to return to it once the war had finished. Then, after the end of the Second World War, a new global kind of Gold Standard – underpinned by the United States and the US dollar – developed. The American government made a promise to convert dollars into gold at a fixed rate, and other countries around the world agreed to fix their exchange rates to the dollar, effectively also pegging their currencies to a fixed price of gold. This meant that they needed to have the reserves of dollars to back up those promises – so dollars rather than gold flowed across borders, helping to balance out differences in demand between different economies.

Advocates of the Gold Standard argued that it provided an anchor to the value of currency. President Herbert Hoover, speaking in 1933, said 'we have gold because we cannot trust governments'.[1] He meant that, without the requirement to have gold backing up the currency, governments would be inclined to continually expand the money supply, leading to inflation and a devaluation of the currency itself. Gold acted as a disciplining device, as governments could only increase the money supply if they were able to also acquire additional gold reserves to back it.

However, anyone who has seen the Bond film *Goldfinger* will know this system has some flaws. In the film, the villainous bullion dealer Auric Goldfinger tries to poison much of the United States' gold with radiation, rendering it unusable. His objective is to reduce the gold supply and so boost the value of his own gold holdings (fortunately, he is thwarted by 007 and Pussy Galore). If this was a little far-fetched, it did hint at one of the major problems afflicting the Gold Standard. Changes in the demand and supply of gold would affect its price. These things were largely outside of the control of policymakers, and so couldn't be altered to try to stabilise the economy when there was a recession or an economic boom. Eventually its flaws became sufficiently apparent that the Gold Standard collapsed. First the UK left in 1931. Then, in 1971, US President Richard Nixon officially broke the link between the dollar and gold at a fixed price.

Since the end of the Gold Standard, that 'promise to pay the bearer' on banknotes has become a little more nebulous – it is a promise to exchange it not for gold, but for more banknotes. There is nothing intrinsically valuable, like gold, underpinning the note's worth. Far from being a weakness, this has a number of benefits. First, it makes it possible to vary the supply of money as demand fluctuates. This keeps prices in the economy more stable. Second, it is more efficient. All the time your money is being backed up by something with intrinsic value – that is, something that people want for reasons other than just being money – you're not using that commodity for the thing that people might want it for. Gold being used to back up pieces of money can't be used to make jewellery or computer chips, so it's much better to use something that has very little intrinsic value, which won't be missed.

We call this money without intrinsic value *'fiat'* – meaning 'let it be done' in Latin. This encapsulates the ethos that fiat money is money because it has been deemed so. In practice, this often means a declaration by the government as to what qualifies as money. One economic theory around where money gets its value from says it is derived from the fact that the state allows, or requires, you to pay tax with it – meaning there is a ready-made and reliable demand for that form of money. Everyone has to pay taxes, and so if taxes are paid in a certain type of money then people will be willing to pass it to one another, because they know they can eventually pass it on to the government.

So if the state is the body declaring what is and isn't money, does that mean it's the state that's creating money? Unfortunately, it's not quite that simple. Broadly speaking, there are three types of money in most modern economies, but the vast majority of it is not being directly issued or backed by the state.

The first form of money is banknotes, made by central banks.[2] These do act as a direct claim on the state – the 'promise to pay the bearer' represents a claim on the state's resources, even if all you're laying claim to is more banknotes. This money can be held by anyone in the economy. Notes are passed around from one person to the other, exchanging ownership as they go.

The second form is one that most people will not come across in their day-to-day lives. It is money held by banks to pay one another. They hold this money in accounts with the central bank, much as you or I would hold money on deposit at a high-street bank. This money is known as reserves, or narrow money. Like banknotes, it is a claim directly on the central bank and, implicitly, the state. It can only be held by a small number of banks and financial companies who have access to accounts with a central bank like the Bank of England. Its main use is for banks to clear their debts to one another at the end of each day, a phenomenon that we'll explore in the next chapter.

However, by far the most common form of money – the money we all depend on every day – takes a third form. This money makes up the deposits we have in our bank accounts. They make up 79 per cent of the money supply and 96 per cent of the money used by the general public. But, perhaps shockingly, this form of money is not a claim on the state at all. It is an IOU to a private company. A very specific type of private company – a bank. Most of us use our bank deposits day in, day out without ever thinking about the difference between the note in our pocket and the numbers on our bank statements, but they are not the same.

This is one of the core revelations about money in a modern economy. Most of the money we use every day is not created by the Bank of England, or its counterparts such as the Federal Reserve or the European Central Bank. These central banks do create money; supplying as many banknotes as people in the economy want and providing electronic money to the banking system in the form of reserves. However, the vast majority of the money in the system is created not by the Bank of England, but by commercial banks. To create money, they don't need to print it; they simply write it down on a spreadsheet somewhere.

How can this be so? If you ever find yourself looking at an old economics textbook you might be forgiven for thinking that banks simply take in money from savers then loan that money out to borrowers. This way of thinking about the banking system was called the 'loanable funds model', and it was a mainstay of economic theory for a long time. It was easy to model and it made a lot of intuitive sense. Unfortunately, it missed a lot of the key features of modern money.

In the loanable funds model, banks take in deposits from a pool of savings that people want to put away, then they find ways to distribute those savings around the economy. They are simply intermediaries. But this gets the sequencing of the process the wrong way round; banks don't need to take in deposits to make a loan, they simply add money to your account. It is slightly more technically advanced than typing some extra zeroes into an Excel document, but not by much.

Banks can do this because, on the other side of their books, they have an IOU from you in the form of the loan, so the two balance out. In technical jargon they have a matching increase in assets and liabilities. Meanwhile, you have new money in your account that didn't exist five seconds ago. This happens every time a bank lends on a mortgage, or you use your credit card or take out a business loan.

This also means that the converse is true. When you come to pay back that loan, the reverse happens. The bank cancels your debt, but they also reduce your bank balance, so there is less money in the system. By paying back debt, you have destroyed money.

So what stops banks just creating infinite amounts of money? Well, for one thing they limit themselves. Banks want to be able to make a profit, and that places a limit on how much money they create. They will only give money to people who they think can pay it back in a way that is profitable for the bank. There also need to be people willing to take on that debt at the terms the banks offer. Banks can't force you to take out a loan. At the point banks stop making loans, money creation stops.

But this money creation process is such an integral part of our economic lives that we, as a society, and as policymakers, don't leave it purely in the hands of bankers. Banks are strictly regulated; part of the deal when you get a banking licence is that you will not overstretch yourself beyond your resources. One of the major roles of the Bank of England is in regulating how much money commercial banks are able to bring into circulation and making sure they only do so in a safe and sustainable way. And there are other levers that policymakers can pull to limit the amount of money in circulation. By influencing the level of interest rates in the economy, central banks affect how much households and companies want to borrow. We'll learn more about both the levers that the Bank of England can pull in the chapters to come. Stay tuned.

The more entrepreneurial among you may now be thinking, if banks simply create money out of nothing, why can't I get in on that action too? The truth is, anyone can create money. There is nothing to stop you from getting a piece of paper, or a rock, or some computer code and saying 'this is money' and trying to pay with it. The American economist Hyman Minsky once said, 'anyone can create money, the problem is to get it accepted'.[3]

In 2008 an anonymous computer scientist (or scientists)[4] going by the name of Satoshi Nakamoto released a paper titled 'Bitcoin: a peer-to-peer electronic cash system'. Nakamoto's dream was to invent a new form of money that was completely independent from central authorities: central banks, governments and even commercial banks. Instead, trust in the currency would come from the underlying technology – called a blockchain – which meant that transactions between people were verified collectively, based on checks and balances in the computer code itself. As well as offering a form of anonymity to its users, the overall supply was determined right at the start, hardwired into the code. No governments, central banks or commercial banks could create more out of thin air for their own needs. The underlying code means that the supply of the new currency – Bitcoin – will increase until around 2041, when the total supply hits 21 million bitcoins. Then there can be no more.

By the start of 2009 Nakamoto had launched his (or their) idea in practice and Bitcoin was born. The timing was impeccable, offering an alternative just at the point the 2007–8 financial crisis was destroying confidence in banks and the status quo. The very first block of Bitcoin had coded in a reference to a headline in *The Times* from January 2009, saying 'Chancellor on the brink of second bailout for banks', just to hammer the point home.[5]

Now, more than a decade later, Bitcoin has been on a remarkable journey. Its price has soared and then crashed, soared and then crashed, many times over. It has moved from a niche conversation among computer nerds to dinner-party talk around the world. It has become Twitter fuel for tech billionaires and politicians alike, and generated more Reddit threads than videos of cats playing with babies.[6]

Nakamoto has certainly created something that has captured the public imagination, and that has wide appeal. But did he, in fact, create a new form of money? The answer for most economists is: probably not, at least in Bitcoin's current form. To understand why, we must return to what it means to be money, and the functions laid out by Adam Smith a quarter of a millennium ago.

First, those price moves. Bitcoin is ten times more volatile than most major exchange rates. Those huge swings in prices have made some people very rich. But if someone who owed you £100 offered you a piece of paper that tomorrow could either be worth £200 or 10p, would you take it? Maybe for a gamble, but not for your day-to-day spending. How do you plan on that basis? This means Bitcoin fails as a store of value. Its worth fluctuates far too much.

Second, few people set their prices in Bitcoin – so it is not the unit of account, at least not outside of a few corners of the internet. Some stores will accept Bitcoin for certain things, but they are working on an exchange rate to existing fiat currencies. They ultimately want to convert that Bitcoin back to pounds sterling, or to US dollars, so they work out how many Bitcoin is equal to the amount of national currency they want. But most people don't want to be thinking about global currency markets when they pop to the shops. Even in El Salvador, where Bitcoin became an officially recognised currency in 2021, it is on price tags alongside US dollars, which have proven themselves to be a far more stable way of storing your purchasing power.

Lastly, it is a pretty poor medium of exchange. This is partly because of the two points above: why would people buy and sell using a currency that fluctuates wildly in value, and isn't accepted everywhere? But it is also because of its more practical limitations. Transactions are much slower than traditional technologies, and the system has struggled to handle the volume of transactions that would be demanded of it as a global payments system. Add to that the huge energy costs and associated environmental impact built in as part of its design – in order to 'mine' new Bitcoin, millions of computer servers have to crunch billions of numbers using terrawatts of electricity – and you have a less than ideal combination.

The other difficulty of Bitcoin is part of what makes it so special to many, including Nakamoto. The fixed supply of Bitcoin means it is equivalent to a Gold Standard, just without the underlying gold. The constraint on the would-be money printer is the computer code. But, as history showed us with the Gold Standard, such rigid supply makes it impossible to react to changes in demand through time. It can lead to significant volatility in prices (inflation) and economic performance. Bitcoin is undoubtedly a fascinating technology, and it has made a lot of people a lot of money, but most economists agree that it isn't money itself.

Bitcoin is only the latest and most high-profile demonstration of the difficulty of creating 'private' money without the backing of the state. In the United States in the early 1800s there were dozens of 'free banks', all creating their own money. More than 90 per cent of notes in circulation in 1830 were private notes issued by banks. But ultimately this system proved inefficient. People didn't trust notes from banks further away than their very local area, making it hard to travel with them. Ultimately, the system simplified down to a single, nationally dictated form of banknote.

This problem crops up time and again. For example, across the UK there are local community currencies – used in areas ranging from Bristol to Brixton. These currencies are designed to help keep money in the local economy and promote local spending. However, almost all of them struggle to gain purchase, beyond as a slight novelty, because they don't offer a particularly good medium of exchange in the less localised world in which we all live. If all of your spending was done locally, you'd be fine. Imagine, though, that you are a Bristolian deli owner who buys their sausages from Cumberland, their turkeys from Norfolk and their beef from the Highlands. Your suppliers won't accept payment in Bristol pounds because they can't spend it in their area, so you won't accept it from your local foodie out for lunch.

Even with the backing of the state, it can be hard for currencies to develop the level of trust they need to get going. Scottish banknotes are not a direct claim on the Bank of England – they are privately issued, much like the notes issued by banks in nineteenth-century America. However, they do have to be backed one-for-one by money held at the Bank of England. To make this possible, the Bank's vaults contain notes called Giants, each worth £1 million, and Titans, each worth £100 million. That means that, should someone holding a Scottish banknote ever want to convert it into a UK sterling note, they can have complete confidence that the bank that issued it has the sterling funds there to back up that promise to pay. And yet, as any Scot travelling south of the border will tell you, there is a suspicion and a hesitancy to accept Scottish banknotes in other parts of the UK. Even though they are, in theory, more securely backed by the British state than deposits in your bank account, people are still unsure about them.

This shows the importance, and complex nature, of trust around money. Money is ultimately a system of mutually agreed trust; over the centuries, people have looked to reinforce that trust in various ways: drawing on the 'intrinsic' value of precious metals and commodities, drawing on the resources and power of the state, or even drawing on the cool logic of computer code. Sometimes these methods work, sometimes they don't. But in every case the goal – explicit or implicit – has been to reinforce people's faith that the money really does have value.

All this gives us a clear sense of what money is now. But don't assume this is the way money will always look. If the history of money tells us anything, it is that the precise nature of money adapts to the world and society around it. If you're reading this book a few years after we wrote it, money might have changed again.

Take the effect the digital world could have on money. We have already become a much more digitised society, with the use of physical cash for transactions on a long-term decline. This trend accelerated in the Covid-19 pandemic, which saw more people switching to using contactless payment and online shopping as they looked to minimise their social and physical contact with others. At the time of writing, cash use in the UK has fallen by 70 per cent in a decade and around half in the last three years. And this all raises a question for institutions like the Bank of England. Do central banks want to join the world of digital money too?

Up until the mid-2010s, all Bank of England staff had a perk: the option of bank accounts at the Bank of England itself. They had the privilege of being able to hold money directly on the central bank's books, as well as the honour of having the sort-code 10–00–00. Most only held small balances in these accounts, as much a badge of honour as a practical decision. They could usually get better returns on their money in a commercial bank – and if anyone should trust the safety of the banking system, it is the people charged with looking after it.

Unfortunately, this perk is now gone. The final accounts closed in 2017. But now, once again, a variation of this system has become a real possibility. Technological developments over the last twenty years mean that it would now be feasible for the central bank to offer accounts not just to its employees, but to everyone in the economy. This is the essence of what central bankers call central bank digital currency. It would be a way for the majority of people to hold a direct claim on the state, but in a digital form, without having to hold huge amounts of banknotes or to rely on an IOU from the banking system.

The idea is in its early stages, but it could represent the biggest change to money in centuries. Perhaps one of the biggest changes it would bring is that money from a central bank could, possibly, pay interest.[7] Milton Friedman was among a number of economists to point out the economic inefficiency that arose from keeping hold of your paper money – the fact that it doesn't pay interest. As we'll learn in the next chapter, one of the great benefits of commercial banks is that they do pay interest – when you keep money with them, you get that money and a little more back. Not so if you're holding cash. As a result, you are losing value on your wealth when you hold it in money.

This has intriguing economic consequences: because prices are constantly going up, people try to reduce the amount of paper money they hold to reduce the loss they make. Writing in a world where there wasn't the technology to charge interest on banknotes, Friedman's solution was to bring inflation down to be the same as the interest rate on a note – zero.

However, thanks to technological advances in the last few decades, we could now conceivably have a digital banknote that paid you interest. A central bank digital currency could combine the features of a banknote, like it being a direct claim on the central bank rather than a private business, with the ability to pay interest, like a bank deposit. This interest rate could be set by the central bank directly, meaning that people who held balances in a Bank of England account could get rewarded in a way they don't for banknotes. This would remove the cost to holding money, and mean people held a more efficient amount of it.

Another big change that a central bank digital currency would bring would be to offer people many of the conveniences of a bank account without having to use a commercial bank. The vast majority of us hold our money in the form of digital balances with a high street bank. One of the main reasons is that we want to make digital payments – buy things online, transfer the money from one account to the next – and physical money isn't well suited to that. In the current system, though, digital payments can only be made with money created by the private sector, predominantly banks – so people living a digital life have no choice but to step away from state-backed money. Regulation and government schemes that guarantee deposits held at banks make this private money remarkably safe. But as we'll learn in the next chapter, some people may still feel the banking system contains more risk than they would like to take on. They would prefer to have money directly backed by the state. This is something a central bank digital currency could offer.

Of course, there are always risks with big changes, and one of the main risks that economists will have to solve before embarking on any form of digital currency is what happens to the old forms of money. If everyone holds their money in central bank digital currency and no one holds deposits with their banks any more, what happens to the banking sector? As we'll explore in the next chapter, commercial banks perform a crucial role in keeping the economy running smoothly.

Whether the risk outweighs the benefits, and whether people will even want a central bank digital currency, remains to be seen. But money has always evolved with the times, and it will continue to do so. It meets the needs and desires of the society it serves. If demand for a state-backed, digital form of money exists, that may be what we get. Perhaps before long, the staff of Threadneedle Street will get their old internal bank accounts back – as will the rest of the world. You too could have the sort code 10–00–00.

So what is money, all told? There are a few ways to answer the question. On one level, money is anything and everything that we decide it is – gold coins and banknotes, precious rocks and old teeth, cigarettes and mackerels. As soon as everyone can agree that something is money, then money it becomes.

In practice, though, some things lend themselves better to being money than others. So on the next level, money needs to fulfil three central criteria – first outlined by Adam Smith in the eighteenth century. It must be a medium of exchange, it must carry a store of value both now and in the future, and it must be a unit of account. These qualities mean that, in general, coins are a better vehicle for money than mackerel is.

In the modern world, the answer to the question is more complicated again. Surprisingly, money is largely a system of IOUs issued by private companies, not a claim on the state or a promise of gold. The bulk of the money we use every day, in the form of bank deposits, is nothing more than a promise by our bank to pay us back, created out of thin air when they lend. However, the trust in money remains because the state regulates and monitors the process of money creation – to ensure it is undertaken responsibly.

And that, at the highest level, is what money is: a system of trust. It works because everyone thinks it's going to work. I trust that this £5 note is worth £5, and so do you. And who maintains that trust? First, the Bank of England and other central banks. And second, other banks. These institutions play a crucial role in maintaining trust and creating the money we need to keep the economy, and our daily lives, moving.

But this is not all that banks do. They perform a range of other vital roles in the modern economy. In the process, they also bring the potential for great economic fragility. To understand how the economy works (and sometimes doesn't work), we need to learn about the banking system.

Chapter Eight
Why shouldn't I hoard all my money under the mattress?

On the benefits of banking, why your money should be safer in a bank than ever before, and how to avoid accidentally binning all your savings.

In 2009, a woman in Israel decided to surprise her mother by buying her a new mattress. It was a generous gift, likely rooted in a concern for her mum's back. As the old mattress was driven off to a tip in Tel Aviv, the daughter proudly presented her mother with a newer, comfier model.

Unfortunately, her mother had been holding on to the old mattress for a reason. It was lined with $1 million in cash – her mother's life savings. Over the course of the next week, the daughter would dash between three tips across Tel Aviv looking for the mattress and the cash, to no avail.[1] The money was lost.

Although losing millions of dollars of cash might be relatively rare, examples of people hoarding cash in this way are quite common. Many of us know older relatives who keep large amounts of cash – certainly far more than they're ever likely to need for their day-to-day spending – in a drawer in the kitchen or back bedroom.

Why is this kind of cash-hoarding so widespread? The answer, perhaps, is that it is a very normal and human instinct – particularly in times of economic turmoil. At the beginning of the coronavirus crisis, many people began hoarding cash in a similar way to toilet roll. According to a Bank of England survey, during the Covid-19 crisis in 2020 nearly one in ten people started to hoard extra cash as a precaution.[2] This was hardly the first time, either. In 2020, a haul of 1,069 silver coins was discovered in Suffolk; archaeologists speculated that they had been stashed for safe-keeping during the English Civil War in the seventeenth century.[3] These decisions have often been rooted in a mistrust of banks. The unfortunate Israeli woman who lost her savings had been hoarding the $1 million in the wake of the 2007–8 financial crisis, perhaps because she had lost trust in the banking industry. She was not alone in this: two-thirds of people said they didn't trust banks in a 2018 YouGov survey.[4]

So why shouldn't you hoard your money under (or inside) a mattress? The shortest answer is to avoid the situation the woman in our Israeli case study found herself in: banks can keep your money safe. But that's not all banks are good for. When you store your money in a bank, it's to your benefit and everyone else's. Banks let you freely move your money around an economy; they pay you interest; and at the level of the entire economy, they make sure that money is being efficiently used. And while people can be forgiven for having some misgivings about banks – they've had their share of controversies – there are all sorts of measures in place to make sure that your cash is secure when you deposit it.

In short, bank accounts are just about good for everyone. They are much more than a place to store money. They are crucial to the operation of the entire global economy.

In around 2000 BCE, some entrepreneurial Babylonian priests spotted a business opportunity. Between worshipping their several thousand deities, they somehow found time to start storing people's gold for a fee – usually extracted by taking a fraction of the gold being stored. For the most part, this gold sat idle in the basement of temples for long periods, gathering dust alongside statues of gods and goddesses until the owners wanted it back. As time went on, this system subtly changed. By the eighteenth century BCE, the priests had started to loan out the gold they were protecting to others who needed it. After all, most people storing their gold in the temple didn't need it all the time, so why not share some of it around? These business-savvy priests didn't realise it, but they had created what is now perhaps the most important business in the world. These temples were arguably the world's first banks.

The idea soon caught on. With time, priestly financiers became a staple in parts of Greece and later the Roman Empire. Soon, instead of just storing gold in temples, people were constructing buildings dedicated to storing and lending out money – precursors to the banks of today. This world of early finance boomed until the collapse of the Roman Empire, at which point the banks closed shop. But the basic model of the banking industry had been established.

It would be almost a millennium before such banks would properly re-emerge. But in the twelfth and thirteenth centuries, money dealers began popping up on the streets of Lombardy, in Italy. They became known for the small wooden benches from which moneylenders would operate. This is where the word 'banks' comes from – the Italian for bench, *banca*. The word 'bankruptcy' has a similar origin; when the moneylender ran out of money, some benches would be broken in half and would have to cease doing business. They would be declared *banca rotta* – a rotten bench.

Initially these lenders offered loans to farmers who wanted to borrow money to buy grain. However, this was considered risky as the farmers might not have paid back the loan, so moneylenders asked that the farmers give them some of their harvest to compensate them: they charged interest. As well as lending, the money dealers soon started holding deposits of money for their customers. These deposits of money were at first intended to be held in case the harvest failed, but often they were used for the bench's own trades.

Soon these businesses became more sophisticated. By the fifteenth century, banks had become places where people could deposit their money in exchange for a note that promised the holder the amount they had deposited. This was essentially a 'bill of exchange', which we would now recognise as a banknote. And no longer were they limited to Italy: by the seventeenth century, banks were common across Europe, from Barclays in England to Berenberg in Germany. Naturally, the exchange was not just about money, but also about power. Many of those humble Lombardy benches would develop into banks for European royals who needed money to pay for wars. Some would become 'central banks', created to offer loans to the state – like the Bank of England, founded in 1694.

Over the next 350-odd years, the number and scale of these banks would increase beyond recognition, and yet the basic model – an institution that offers loans, backed up by some kind of financial reserve – has remained largely unchanged since the sixteenth century. Today, banks come in myriad shapes and sizes – from investment banks in the City of London to those lending to consumers, either on the high street or via an app on your phone. But each fundamentally has the same key functions, ones that a Lombard clerk on a Renaissance *banca* may well have recognised.

We'll start with the obvious ones. The first key function of banks remains to store money. The average person in the UK in 2021 had more than £5,000 in their bank savings accounts.[5] Without banks they would have to store it in their house or give it to someone they trust to look after it. Not ideal. It would be a hassle, you might lose it, and every time you left the house you might worry about it being stolen. Instead, we choose banks to store most of our money for us. This is perhaps the most ancient function of banks – pioneered by those Babylonian priests in 2000 BCE.

Here at the Bank of England, like any other bank, we store money. Deep underground in the vaults in our head office in Threadneedle Street are rows and rows of brand-new £5, £10, £20 and £50 banknotes, ready to be distributed when they are needed. But our vaults are better known as a place of safekeeping for something else: gold. We look after gold for governments and some other central banks. It is a job that the Bank of England has been doing for more than 300 years. Today there are around 400,000 bars of gold worth over £200 billion stored in the Bank's vaults. This amounts to a fifth of all the gold in the world. If stacked all on top of each other, it would reach the height of forty-six Eiffel Towers. This gold covers over 300,000 square feet – equivalent to almost ten football pitches.

The second function of banks is similarly straightforward: they allow us to pay for the things we need. Banks mean you don't have to carry around all the cash you think you might need in your bag that day, and, crucially, it's possible to transport money from one bank branch to another. You don't need to visit the bank where you have deposited your money, or the one nearest to your house every time you need to get money out or pay for something.

To make this possible, modern banks draw on a sprawling system designed to make payments easy. Think of debit cards. Nearly all adults in the UK own debit cards and use them for day-to-day payments.[6] Transactions like these add up. In the UK there are over £8 million worth of money transactions made per second – £700 billion worth of exchanges between bank accounts every single day. All these individuals and businesses hold accounts with different banks. Because of the overwhelming quantity of these transactions, banks don't usually move money between each other in real time – instead, they keep a tally in their computer systems and settle up what they owe each other at the end of the day. This is called settlement and is completed in the UK via the Bank of England, which is one of our most important roles as a central bank. Many banks have accounts with the Bank of England, which allows them to transfer money to other banks. In 2020, the Bank of England processed nearly £92 trillion of payments. The economic benefit of this role of banks is difficult to overstate. If banks didn't provide a way for you to pay others, it could cause the economy to grind to a halt. By having a system to settle these payments, the risk of someone not being paid on time is eliminated.

Then there's the third function of banks: they match borrowers to savers. Banks act as middlemen between people who want to save money and people who want money to spend. In principle, we don't need banks to do this – everyone could just borrow money from friends or family members. But this could cause problems. First, you may not know anyone who has spare money lying around, especially large sums of it. Second, even if you have rich friends with a lot of spare cash, they might not be willing to lend it to you – not because they're a bad friend, but because they're unsure whether you would be able or willing to pay it back.

Economists call this 'asymmetric information': one person knows more about something than the other. We saw it in Chapter Two as a form of market failure, using the example of the power imbalance between a second-hand car dealer and buyer. In this case, you know more about what you're going to spend the money on and your ability to pay it back than your friend who is lending you the money. In the course of working out whether to lend people money, banks have become masters at overcoming the perils of asymmetric information. They specialise in being able to distinguish between the good loans and the potentially bad loans, by gathering as much information about people as they can.

Over time, banks have developed various methods to do this. For most of the twentieth century, someone in a suit would have tried to work out whether you were trustworthy enough to pay back a loan – by interviewing you, and perhaps even asking your friends and family. But in recent years, everything has got more sophisticated. Now computers use a large range of information about you and your spending habits to work out whether you'll pay back a loan. They look at information from how much you pay for gym membership to your spending habits in the pub.

Banks are better than the rest of us at doing this, not only because they have greater expertise in assessing the risk, but because they have more information. They get to see your spending habits, monthly income and outgoings in a way the general public does not. By taking all this information into account, banks have an informational advantage and are more efficient lenders than any individual could ever be.

Once they've worked out the likelihood of you paying them back, banks determine the rate of interest they're going to charge you. Just like those Lombard *banchi* of yore, today's banks don't lend for free. Their fee is the price of borrowing money – interest charged on the loan. The interest rate reflects a whole range of things: for instance, the level of risk the bank takes in lending the money. Generally speaking, the bigger the risk, the higher the interest.

You might think that the benefits of this third function of banks are limited to two parties: those receiving a loan, and the bank. But this underestimates the enormous economic importance of lending. By matching savers with the right borrowers, banks put idle money to use and ensure it gets spent in the most productive way possible. When they use their expertise to find the most trustworthy borrowers, banks also – inadvertently – work out who will use it efficiently. Because, luckily for the rest of us, the borrowers who are most likely to pay back their loan tend to be same borrowers who invest it in productive projects. They generate a good return, which can then be used for repaying the loan they received.

So matching savers to borrowers is a socially important task, as well as a way of making money. Banks' most crucial role is funnelling money to where it can be most productive – and so stimulating the economy, while also making a profit for themselves. Along the way, banks have another effect: they cause more money to circulate in the system. To understand how, we need to jump through time again – this time to mid-seventeenth-century England.

Against a backdrop of rising political tensions between King Charles I and his Parliament, many wealthy families at the time looked for somewhere to store their gold. That's where London's goldsmiths came in handy. They offered wealthy Londoners a service: they could deposit their gold in the vaults and the goldsmiths would issue receipts clarifying the quantity and purity of the metal. These receipts could then be used to collect the stored gold when the owners wanted it back. The goldsmiths' great innovation, however, was deciding not to just sit on the gold. They realised they could lend it out to others in return for a fee, provided they made sure it was returned before the original owner wanted it back. Some of this fee was given to people storing the original gold, to compensate them on the off-chance the gold wasn't returned. This was a tool that our ancient priests had also used, but in the seventeenth century it would become much more widespread.

By loaning out the gold, they could earn more money than just by storing it. This process also allowed them to fund a higher number of productive investments than if they kept all the gold in their vaults, which generated an economic boost. This return on investment could then be reinvested elsewhere, generating even more return and investment, which in turn stimulated the economy. Even better, some of the money made from this process came back to the goldsmiths-cum-bankers as a deposit – who could then loan it out to someone else. The cycle continued: more money being loaned led to more economic activity, which led to more money being loaned. The eagle-eyed among you will have noticed that this essentially led to more money in the system.

Nowadays modern banks have taken this magical process of creating money a step further. As we saw in the previous chapter, money in most economies is no longer backed by gold: banks are able to create more of it out of thin air.

But goldsmiths in the seventeenth century and banks today have still a lot in common; they both convert short-term deposits – the gold or cash that people hold in their accounts – into long-term lending of money. This process is known as 'maturity transformation'. Through this process, banks benefit themselves, savers, borrowers and others in the economy – leading to more and more productive economic output.

So far, so good. The only problem is if those goldsmiths – or our modern bankers – were to lend too much money. It wouldn't be a good look if customers went to take their gold out of the vaults, only to be told that it had been lent out – and the goldsmith had no way of getting it back until the recipient of the loan paid up. The goldsmiths' solution, which is still used by bankers to this day, was to keep some gold in their vaults: they hold a fraction of it in reserve.

This mechanism is known as fractional reserve banking. In the seventeenth century, it meant that if a few people were late to bring back the gold they borrowed, or others wanted their gold back earlier than expected, our goldsmiths were always able to give it to them. Today it means that all banks keep a certain amount of real or virtual cash in their vaults, to limit the risk of running out of money. The big question, then, is how much cash banks should have to hold.

In the early 1930s, six American economists came up with a dramatic proposal. It rested on a very simple idea: banks should be able to pay back their depositors all of what they were owed at any point in time. The proposal was known as the Chicago Plan, because its main advocates were based at the University of Chicago.[7]

This proposal ran counter to the most basic logic of modern banking, as it had been practised since the days of those London goldsmiths. In a fractional reserve system, banks always give out more money than they have in their vaults. This, the Chicago economists suggested, was a problem. They argued that it made the banking system inherently fragile. There was a tension between the two roles that banks play whenever they lend: both creating money that will circulate in the economy and allocating money from savers to borrowers.

Where was the tension? In the fact that if everyone who had deposited their money in a bank demanded it back at once, the whole system would collapse: not just a few banks, but the whole process through which money entered circulation. This is because a fractional reserve bank will only have, by definition, a fraction of all deposits that could possibly be demanded. This fragility, the Chicago economists claimed, had been laid bare by the economic crash of 1929 (more on that in the next chapter).

The Chicago economists' solution was to separate out these two functions, leaving money creation to the government and credit allocation to the banks. Any bank must then hold enough money with a central bank to completely cover the deposits that could be withdrawn. They would become 'narrow' banks, meaning there was no gap between what they lent out and what they might have to pay out quickly.

The Chicago Plan gained a lot of traction, and it is still discussed nowadays by economists and international institutions, like the International Monetary Fund, but it never made it into law.[8] Fortunately, on the whole, people don't all demand their money back at once – and so the system remains relatively stable. However, the Chicago Plan's authors did have a point. When you think about it, the modern banking system rests on a paradox. We all believe that banks keep our money safe, and for the most part they do. But if for a moment we all stopped believing that banks are safe – and tried to take that money out – the whole system would collapse. It's like the magic of money we encountered in Chapter Seven: the very act of trusting that the banking system works, makes it work.

And while moments when everyone simultaneously loses that trust are rare, they're not *that* rare. Bank runs, when everyone tries to withdraw their money at once, do happen. Their role in fiction is telling. You might recall the bank run on the Bailey Building and Loan in the 1946 film *It's a Wonderful Life*. It starts just as George Bailey, a newlywed in charge of his family's small bank, sets off for his honeymoon, only to discover that depositors have gathered outside his bank demanding their money.

Bank runs can be triggered by rumours, and this fictional one isn't any different. The people of Bedford Falls have heard rumours that Bailey Building and Loan had asked to borrow money from another bank because some of its own borrowers weren't able to make payments. As the angry punters demand their money, George explains that he can't give everyone their deposits as they are being loaned out to other customers.

Alas, such situations are not confined to heart-warming Christmas films. *It's a Wonderful Life* might have felt eerily prophetic to anyone who lived through the 2007–8 financial crisis. In September 2007, queues of people began to grow outside the British bank Northern Rock seeking to withdraw all their money at once. The bank run had been triggered by reports on BBC News that Northern Rock had run into financial problems, and was looking to borrow money from the Bank of England.

Within three days of the report, Northern Rock would be the victim of the first bank run in the UK since the nineteenth century. Many people queued for several hours. As more people heard the news of the bank run, they got worried and decided to join the queue. Even if there is only a very small chance of the bank not being able to give you your money back, there is a very strong incentive to make sure you are among the first to withdraw it – before the bank is unable to return your deposits. The longer you wait, the more you think you risk losing everything. Between them, these individual decisions became a self-fulfilling prophecy, with every new person who joined the queue increasing the likelihood of Northern Rock running short of cash.

This was, in many respects, quite rational behaviour. At the time, deposit insurance – known in the UK as the Financial Services Compensation Scheme – only guaranteed that customers would get paid back £2,000 of their deposits and then 90 per cent of the next £33,000 if Northern Rock failed. It made perfect sense for people with large savings to join the queue in 2007. Today, you'll be glad to hear, the insurance scheme guarantees that all deposits under £85,000 will be paid back no matter what happens to a bank.

But bank runs can still happen. And history shows that, when they do, they can be catastrophic. In *It's a Wonderful Life*, George's wife steps in and uses their honeymoon money to pay angry customers, saving the Bailey Building and Loan from bankruptcy but ruining their holiday. Unfortunately, many banks don't have enough honeymoon cash lying around to save them. During the Great Depression of the 1930s, in the US 7,000 banks collapsed between 1929 and 1933 – many triggered by bank runs just like that on Bailey Building and Loan.[9]

So what do bankers do if they see a queue of angry customers forming outside their doors, all wanting to take their money out? They might turn to their own bank for help. And in the UK the bank to the bankers is us, the Bank of England. Central banks are known as 'lenders of last resort'. They are there for banks when they get into trouble, like when they don't have enough cash to hand to pay their depositors.

There are conditions, of course. Only in certain circumstances will central banks lend to struggling commercial banks. The first person to codify these terms was Walter Bagehot, one of those polymathic, heavily bearded Victorian gentlemen with a strong view on almost everything.[10] Between editing *The Economist* and writing a seminal work of constitutional theory, *The English Constitution*, Bagehot found time to write the definitive book on central banking: *Lombard Street*.

The book took its name from the street on which Overend, Gurney and Company, a moneylender, was located in the mid-nineteenth century. It was, and is, also the street behind the Bank of England, which in turn took its name from those innovative Italians behind the earliest *banche*. In May 1866, Overend Gurney, at that point the largest moneylender in the City of London, suspended payments to its customers. Panic ensued, so much so that *The Times* christened the day 'Black Friday' – one of several Black Fridays that would hit the finance industry over the next 150 years.[11]

At that stage in its history, the Bank of England was still a private bank – albeit one with an unusual status. It enjoyed some of the privileges associated with a central bank, such as control of the country's gold reserve and a monopoly over the issuance of banknotes in London. It also offered emergency loans at cheap rates to other banks. This time, however, its board refused assistance to Overend Gurney, thinking the company couldn't be saved. The board concluded that its financial woes had been caused by a series of bad business decisions, which led it to take on much greater risk than it should have. Instead of saving Overend Gurney, the Bank of England offered support to other banks and brokers, depleting its own reserves to do so. In the process, the Bank ensured that other moneylenders didn't also fail, nor did the whole financial system come crashing down.

Bagehot praised the Bank of England for accepting its role as lender of last resort. He used the incident to outline in what circumstances such lenders should act. The former Deputy Governor at the Bank of England, Paul Tucker, summarised Bagehot's dictum: 'to avert panic, central banks should lend early and freely (i.e. without limit), to solvent businesses, against good collateral, and at "high rates"'.[12] This essentially means that during a panic, central banks should only lend to banks that will, in time, be able to recoup the loans they have made, and carry on providing bank services to their customers. What's more, if an emergency loan is made, it should be done at sufficiently high interest rates to discourage other banks from turning to the central bank for help unless absolutely necessary.

In this rendering, central banks are a little like economic seat belts. They'll protect you in certain circumstances but not all. Seat belts will help protect you when you've been hit by another car, or maybe if you're caught in an unexpected storm that's blown you off course. But if you're just a bad driver, they cannot continually protect you from your own reckless behaviour. Likewise, central banks will only tide over a struggling bank for a short period of time, for example until the loans they have made have been paid back. Central banks can't save banks that have made loans that turn out to be bad, or banks that have overstretched themselves in other ways – by spending too much on salaries, for example.

All this means that judging when to step in is a tricky call. Central banks have to be careful who they lend to and on what terms. To understand why, let's return to seat belts. The economist Samuel Peltzman – yet another professor at the University of Chicago – once argued that mandating seat-belt use would lead to an increase in the number of car accidents. He reasoned that seat belts would make people think they were safe to take greater risks: they could drive however recklessly they liked, wrongly thinking the seat belt would save them if things went wrong. He called this 'risk compensation'.[13] This theory turned out to be incorrect, at least in the UK, where the number of road injuries declined immediately upon the introduction of compulsory seat belts in 1983.[14] But it does, perhaps, have some relevance in the financial world. If banks knew they had a central bank on standby to help them out without strict conditions, why wouldn't they take a few more risks in pursuit of getting more customers (and generating higher profits)?

Economists call this excessive risk-taking when you know you'll be bailed out 'moral hazard'. To reduce moral hazard on the road, the economist Gordon Tullock once argued that instead of mandating seat belts, the government should require large spikes to be installed in the centre of steering wheels – known as Tullock spikes.[15] These spikes would make drivers more aware of the danger of driving too fast. The Bank of England doesn't quite do that. Instead, to reduce moral hazard in the banking world, central banks place conditions on their lending to commercial banks. And they try to ensure that banks are sufficiently well run that the likelihood of them running into problems is low. This is the purpose of banking regulations and supervision – a set of rules that banks must follow if they are going to be allowed to operate.

These rules include limits on the amount commercial banks can lend out. They also involve a requirement that banks set aside some emergency funds against every loan, to provide a cushion against losses in case some of the loans don't get paid back. These emergency funds are called bank capital – the difference between what a bank owns and what it owes. You can think of it as a protective buffer to make sure a bank can afford to lose money on its loan without going bust. It comes from the bank's share-holders. If you buy £100 of shares in a bank, then you are providing it £100 of capital. If the bank does badly and makes losses, you will lose some or all of that money. If the bank does well, you will be entitled to a portion of its profits, paid to you as a share dividend.

It is now widely accepted that before the 2007–8 financial crisis, banks had too little capital – a view shared by everyone from the economist Joseph Stiglitz to former US president Barack Obama. But since then central banks and regulators have introduced a wave of new policies to increase capital and reduce moral hazard. Now UK banks have more than three times more capital than before the crisis.[16]

Is this enough capital to ensure your money is safe with the bank? Given how bad banking crises can be shouldn't the Bank of England set even higher capital requirements to ensure that banks never fail? The issue is, just like placing a spike on the steering wheel might mean no one would want to drive, placing too high a capital requirement on banks would stop them from lending and fulfilling their other useful economic functions – thus making the economy and everyone in it worse off.

Instead of just endlessly ramping up capital requirements for everyone, today's central banks tend to take a more flexible approach. Capital requirements can vary. Think of them as speed limits, changing from road to road but always designed to stop drivers taking too many risks. For one thing, banks that make riskier loans are required to have more capital, while banks that make safer loans are required to have less. Since the 2007–8 financial crisis, central banks have introduced new 'macro-prudential policies', which determine how much capital banks have to hold depending on economic and credit conditions: that is, how easy it is for people to get loans.

When credit conditions are bad – and so banks are reluctant to lend – they are required to hold less capital. When credit conditions are good – and banks are happy to give out loans – they are required to hold more. This is meant to encourage banks to build capital 'buffers', designed to cushion them when the economy is strong; they can then reduce these buffers, and continue lending, during times of economic turbulence. The reasoning is that when times are tough, banks might be tempted to stop giving out loans, which would lead to even more economic trouble. In these moments, policymakers want banks to keep lending, so they are allowed to have a smaller protective buffer, and are therefore more likely to continue to lend. When the economy is doing well, on the other hand, it makes sense for banks to have a more substantial protective buffer, so that if things do start to go wrong, they have money to hand. This principle – that when the economy is doing badly banks' capital can be lower, and vice versa – is called the countercyclical capital buffer.

Here in Britain, the size of this buffer is set by the Financial Policy Committee at the Bank of England, which consists of the Governor and a number of senior economists from within and outside the Bank. Whenever conditions in the economy change, the Committee considers changing the size of the buffer. For example, as the coronavirus crisis swept across the globe in March 2020, the Committee reduced the amount of capital banks had to hold. This helped to ensure banks were able to continue lending money even when the economy was looking shaky, and fewer people seemed likely to pay them back.

How does the Bank of England know where to set these capital requirements? In large part, it's down to economic modelling – which we'll learn about in the next chapter. But central bankers have a few other tricks up their sleeve. Sometimes, central banks decide how much capital banks have to hold by stimulating a 'stress test'. They model an economic crisis and ask banks to show them how they would respond. The banks have to say what they would do if, for example, GDP were to fall by 10 per cent: how would this affect their lending and how much capital they hold? How big would losses on mortgages be if the unemployment rate rose by, say, five percentage points? These simulations help policymakers come to decisions on how much capital banks should be holding.

This all sounds helpful in theory. Of course, such policies are fairly meaningless without the power to back them up. And that's why central banks don't just set the rules of the road – they have financial traffic officers to impose them. In the UK, the Prudential Regulation Authority, part of the Bank of England, and the Financial Conduct Authority, an independent regulatory body, are those officers. They are responsible for making sure the banks are sticking to regulations. If they aren't, they can be slapped with a hefty fine or, in extreme cases, be stopped from operating at all. Another element of this traffic-officer role is trying to keep things orderly when they do go wrong. When banks do fail, central banks have a process known as 'resolution' to ensure they do so safely without harming customers, other banks or the rest of the financial system.

These changes are all relatively new. They were implemented in the wake of the financial crisis of 2007–8, at which point the public and policymakers realised that the banking sector needed to be more resilient to economic shocks. But their results have been significant. They mean that your money should be safer in a bank now than ever before – and certainly safer than if you hoarded it under that mattress.

As employees of the Bank of England, we probably would say that banks are a good thing. Fortunately, we're not alone in making this case: pretty much all economists agree that banks aren't just the safest place to store your money – they're integral to the functioning of the global economy.

That's down, most obviously, to the economic benefits to individuals of keeping their money in bank accounts. It's safer – the money in your mattress can get thrown away or stolen, as it can in banks, but it's less likely. At the same time, money stored in banks is easier to use – you can withdraw money from a cash machine everywhere from Andorra to Zanzibar without lugging it around in your suitcase. This has an economic benefit that extends far beyond any one person: it keeps money circulating smoothly through the economy.

At the same time, what banks actually do with the money you deposit has a beneficial economic effect. Banks don't just sit on your savings, they lend them out to other people and businesses. Through the fractional reserve system, they lend out much more money than they have in their vaults – in the process creating more money, as we saw in Chapter Seven. By lending out money, banks help channel savings to their most productive uses: for example by lending to individuals so they can buy a house, or to businesses to fund investment.

And, while hesitancy about the risks of banking is a historical constant, today your money is safer in a bank than ever before. There are a whole suite of rules, regulations and capital standards in place to ensure that depositing your money is safe. What's more, the Bank of England's status as 'lender of last resort' means it is on hand if banks encounter short-term cashflow problems. Should things go really badly wrong, the process of resolution is set up to ensure that if banks do fail they can do so safely – without causing a domino effect across the financial system.

In all, banks both keep your money safe and make sure everyone's money is being put to good use across the economy. But even in an age of sophisticated financial regulation, the banking system doesn't always tick over smoothly. Financial problems at banks do happen – in many cases as a result of wider trouble in the economy. Central banks can lessen the consequences of economic crises, and try to stop problems in the financial system from making such crises worse. But they cannot eliminate them entirely. It's these economic crises – and what to do about them – that form the focus of our final two chapters.

Chapter Nine

Why did no one see the crash coming?

On economic crises and their causes, why it's no fun living through recessions, and the surprising similarities between economists and weathermen.

In November 2008, the Queen paid a visit to the London School of Economics to open a new building. Many thought it would be a fairly run-of-the-mill visit. The Queen had other ideas. This being the height of the 2007–8 financial crisis – the worst since the 1930s – the modernist architecture wasn't the only thing on her mind. Part-way through the tour, she turned to the assorted economists and asked a question the rest of the nation was also wondering: 'Why did no one see it coming?'

This is a question that economists would spend the next decade debating. They would talk it over in university lecture halls and economic journals; in broadsheet columns and on TV debates. Meanwhile, the relatively few economists who did see it coming became economic celebrities overnight.

What was the answer? There is a specific one, and a general one. The 2007–8 crisis was fundamentally caused by bad loans made by banks: they had given mortgages to people who had no hope of repaying them. Many (though not all) economists missed it because they didn't join up the dots: realise that just a small number of unpaid loans would have effects far beyond just the housing market because of how intertwined banks were with other parts of the economy. As the LSE economist to whom the Queen had addressed the question, Luis Garicano, later put it in the *Guardian*, 'What I told the Queen is that the reason the situation got out of hand is that those working at every point in the lending chain were eager to continue doing the job they were paid to do.'[1]

The general answer is more complex. It points to the long history of economic crashes, their chaotic nature and their unpredictability. Without fail, there has been an economic crash in each of the last seven decades.

Most famous of all were the events of Thursday 24 October 1929, when the New York Stock Exchange – a market for selling and buying shares in US companies – fell around 10 per cent within the first few hours of opening at 9am.[2] That day would become known as Black Thursday, and would be followed by Black Monday and Black Tuesday a few days later. Within five days, the stock market crashed by 25 per cent.[3] Nearly a century on, Black Monday remains one of the greatest percentage falls on record.

The Wall Street Crash would spark one of the worst economic crises of all time – the Great Depression. The period was followed by mass unemployment and all its attendant woes: spiralling poverty, political unrest, long lines for soup kitchens.[4] This was despite the fact that many New Yorkers, let alone the 526 million people living in Europe at the time, were far removed from the ticker tape and briefcases on Wall Street.[5] What happened on the trading floors of Wall Street impacted the daily lives of not only Americans but millions of people around the world. Global GDP per capita fell by nearly 20 per cent in 1930–2.[6]

Flash forward to 19 October 1987, and on that morning, Wall Street stockbrokers wore similar expressions of surprise and panic on their faces. The stock market spectacularly crashed again, this time by 23 per cent, knocking $1 trillion off the value of the US stock market.[7] This day is commonly known as Black Monday – another one. Many people got flashbacks to 1929: so much so that *Variety* ran the same headline they had on the morning of 30 October 1929: 'Wall Street Lays an Egg'.

Except this time, a crisis in the world of finance didn't spread through the rest of the economy. US GDP growth hit 4 per cent in 1988 and 1989 respectively, and even GDP growth in 1987 was positive overall.[8] It was an economic boom-time.

These two case studies show how complex, unexpected and apparently random financial crises can be. They can come seemingly without warning and can affect just one sector of an economy, or myriad ones. And they also show that financial crises and economic crises are far from the same.

An economic crisis is a contraction in the economy or a fall in GDP – if the economy contracts for more than six months, economists call this a recession. Such crises have a large impact beyond Wall Street, with significant implications for ordinary people's spending and investment decisions. But not all crises in the banking and finance sector lead to economic crises. Only half of those in the financial sector over the past 100 years have resulted in a recession.

So in order to answer the Queen's question, we need to delve into the link between the world of finance and the wider economy. We also need to explain why attempts to predict the trajectory of either are so difficult. There are many times in history when economists have been blindsided by large economic crises, and other times when they haven't happened even when economists thought they would. In fact, economists have been wrong more times than they have been right. Considering all that, how might you embark on the daunting task of predicting the next one?

Over the course of an eighty-five-year life, you're likely to live through eight economic crises. That's double the number of times the average Briton moves house in their lifetime. Your authors have already witnessed two in the UK in the course of our relatively short careers as economists at the Bank of England. But not all of these crises have been world-changing; no two crises are ever the same – the fallout from 1929 was very different to that of 1987, as were each of the thirteen stock-market crashes in the US since. Often the economy gradually expands, then gradually contracts. Sometimes the economy can tank very quickly, then almost immediately recover.

Why do these crises come about? They can be sparked by any number of factors – speculative financial bubbles, bank runs, rises in interest rates, falls in house prices, trade wars, changes in the oil price, wars, famines, social unrest, pandemics or a combination of them all.

But there are a few forms of crisis that are particularly common. Most notably of all, financial crises. Hiccups in the financial world aren't anything new. One of the oldest recorded financial crises was in ancient Rome in 33 CE, when the price of land fell, making it difficult for land-owners who had secured loans against land to pay them back – and causing lenders to stop loaning out money. But in recent decades, problems in the financial system have had wider implications – sometimes leading to full-blown economic crises. This is because financial markets are more integrated into the rest of the economy than ever before, so issues in the financial world can ripple out into other spheres of the economy.

We can make sense of how these financial crises unfold by looking at one of the most famous of these: the South Sea Bubble, which popped in 1720. The South Sea Com-pany had been founded in 1711 to trade with the Spanish colonies in South America, in particular by bringing enslaved Africans to work in mines and on plantations. At the time, Britain was in the midst of a long-running war with Spain, which was costing the UK government a large sum of money. Their solution? To sell government debt to the South Sea Company and issue holders of the debt with shares. The government would then pay annual interest fees to the company's shareholders. The trading company had bribed ministers and MPs to secure this lucrative set-up. By 1720, the company had bought and owned the government's entire £30 million of debt.[9]

As well as being immoral, to the extent it supported the slave trade, this plan was economically problematic. The South Seas were colonies of Spain and Portugal so it would be difficult to make any income from the scheme. Perhaps even more significant than this was the fact that the transatlantic slave trade was an incredibly risky venture – mortality rates on the journey were horrifically high, leading to a loss of human 'property' and therefore profits. While the slave trade could realise large profits for individual investors, on the whole it was far too risky to function as a secure footing for government finance.

Nevertheless, shares in the South Sea Company were in high demand. Everyone from aristocrats and politicians to lower-middle-class Londoners bought shares in the company: investors included the King's mistress, the Duchess of Kendal, and Thomas Pitt, the Earl of Londonderry. Soon the price of South Sea Company shares had soared to nearly £1,000 – equivalent to around £200,000 today.[10] Speculation on these shares was rife; some people bought them knowing they were overpriced, hoping to sell the shares for even higher prices before they returned to a more reasonable level. Some borrowed from banks to buy shares in the company, others invested their life savings. Then, suddenly, the value of the shares plummeted. There was a sudden realisation that the company wasn't worth anything close to the price people were paying for stocks.

This is what economists call a Minsky moment, after Hyman Minsky, who we encountered in Chapter Seven. Semi-forgotten for much of the late twentieth century, Minsky's work was rediscovered in the fallout of the 2007–8 financial crisis. His eponymous moment comes when everyone realises that the shares they have invested in are worth a lot less than they thought.[11] It is the tipping point when speculative activity reaches an extreme that is unsustainable. A particular event may trigger an initial price fall, causing people to panic – in the case of the South Sea Bubble, people realised they were buying shares in a company that wasn't particularly profitable. When you see images of bankers holding their heads in their hands – or, in the case of the South Sea Company, investors staring in dismay at blackboards in London coffee houses – a Minsky moment might be underway.

Even then, this kind of large and sudden fall in the price of shares could bring about a wider economic crisis. In 1720, many people lost their life savings and went bankrupt. Isaac Newton, a savvy investor in his day, lost somewhere in the region of £20,000, or more than £4 million in today's money. He could 'calculate the motions of the heavenly bodies, but not the madness of people', as he later put it.[12] He was describing what economists call herd behaviour: people making decisions based on the behaviour or choices of others.

All these bankruptcies had implications across the economy. Banks in London began to go bust as debts went unpaid. This soon had a deleterious effect on the price of other stocks being bought and sold. Crises of this kind are defined by speculation: massive investment in an asset because people think it will go up in value. When they realise the asset is overvalued, the bubble bursts. It was the same story that would unfold in 1929, 1987 and in 2007–8.

Such speculative bubbles are common, and not all of them result in economic crises. Consider the Great Beanie Baby Bubble. Beanie Babies are soft toys usually worth around $5. In the late 1990s, collectors started to believe that some of the toys were rare and so would only go up in value. And they did, at least for a while. Around this time, one toy sold on eBay for over $5,000, and as the price of these toys rose, more and more people sought them out, increasing the price even more. It was a dramatic era for soft-toy fans. People formed Beanie Babies smuggling rings, a seventy-seven-year-old man (otherwise known as the Beanie Baby Bandit) stole $1,200 worth of toys and a group of children were hurt in a stampede when people rushed to get their hands on a rare 'Garcia' bear. Their manufacturer, Ty, briefly became one of the world's biggest toy companies, and their founder the 877th richest man in the world. But as with most bubbles, what goes up must come down. In 2000, collectors realised the toys were worth a lot less than they had paid for them. This led to many people selling their Beanie Babies, and others who were toying with investing reconsidering their choices, causing the price of these toys to fall even further. Many people lost their savings – one family lost $100,000.[13]

This time, the bubble didn't spill over to wider parts of the economy because it only involved a small number of investors and wasn't linked to other parts of the financial system. However, this does reveal how widespread irrational speculative behaviour is. Such bubbles are very common – in recent years encompassing baseball cards and watches, housing markets and tech company stocks.

Why is speculative behaviour of this kind so wide-spread? The economist Richard Shiller won a Nobel Prize for his explanation. He said that as prices increase, invest-ors want to get in on the action even if it's not rational – a phenomenon he called irrational exuberance. If all your friends are raving about a particular investment – say cryptocurrencies – and they're all saying it will only increase in price, you may be tempted to invest too. It's difficult to believe all your friends could be wrong, so you follow their lead. At the same time, people become more confident when prices are rising, and so less risk-averse. As prices rise, people double down on their investments, which pushes prices even higher.

It would be a mistake to think that speculation is the sole cause of economic crises, though. Consider what economists call 'black swan' events: unpredictable cat-astrophic events that, like black swans, you know exist but are rare and hard to predict in advance. The Covid-19 crisis was a classic black swan. Actions to limit the spread of the virus resulted in shutting down whole economies. National lockdowns were introduced in more than ninety countries, affecting more than half of the global popula-tion. The result was financial panic. On 12 March 2020 the stock market fell by nearly 10 per cent, the worst drop since the 2008 crash.[14]

Given the uncertainty over how long lockdowns would last, and people's fears about new waves and variants, confidence in the economy was low. This meant that even when people could spend their money, a lot of people chose not to. At the same time, many businesses were simply unable to sell their stuff: restaurants and shops closed, factories shuttered themselves, and ships containing exports stopped sailing. It was a perfect storm: a lack of opportunity to spend, combined with a reluctance to do so. During 2020 alone, global GDP fell by nearly 4 per cent, likely the biggest contraction since the Great Depression.[15]

The Covid-19 example shows that speculation is far from the only spark of economic turmoil. Often, crises are caused by obstacles to the effective operation of the global economy. Pandemics, wars, commodity shortages – all make it harder for the economy to function, so can lead to economic turbulence.

Economic crises are expensive. The crisis of 2007–8 cost every single American approximately $70,000, and crises typically cost every Briton £21,000.[16] Enough to buy every woman, man and child in the UK a new Ford Fiesta with some change left over.

In practice, of course, that statistic is only part of the picture. The crisis actually cost some people significantly more than $70,000 and others significantly less. The impact of every crisis varies, affecting different sections of the economy differently – depending on what triggered it and what policies are implemented to counteract it. Some of the impacts may only affect people for short periods of time, while others won't become apparent until years later.

But there are a few recurrent consequences. One of the most immediate economic impacts of a crisis is a fall in confidence in the economy, which means people are less likely to spend money. For example, men are more likely to put off purchasing new underwear during downturns, resulting in a fall in underwear sales during a crisis. This was one of the preferred metrics used by Alan Greenspan, the former head of the US's central bank, the Federal Reserve, to get a feel of how well the economy was performing. The implications of this phenomenon go beyond underwear, however. People tend to cut back their spending during a downturn because assets – such as the their homes – have fallen in price. This makes people feel less wealthy.

This can lead to business closures. Recessions hit all businesses – from large corporations to family-run shops. When people spend less, businesses' revenues fall, making it more difficult to pay costs such as staff wages or electricity bills. If businesses aren't able to pay these costs or borrow money to pay them, they may be forced to shut. Some businesses might cut staff wages to reduce costs and avoid shutting down, but given smaller pay packets, these workers might spend less at other businesses, making it harder for other companies to stay afloat too.

To see how these pressures can ripple across an economy, it's worth paying a visit to Iceland in the late 2000s. Like much of the world, by 2009 the country was in the throes of a huge economic crisis – GDP had fallen by 8 per cent and suddenly the Icelandic krona was worth 50 per cent of what it had been a year previously.[17] Because of the poor exchange rate, McDonald's in Iceland was unable to import the beef, cheese and vegetables needed for its burgers. Suddenly, it was near impossible to run a viable fast-food business. As a result, all three of the McDonald's in Reykjavik had to close down, never to open again. Today, you can visit (or livestream) the country's last remaining Big Mac and fries – enshrined in an airtight glass case in a museum in South Iceland. The streamed Big Mac hints at the long-term fallout of economic crises: many businesses shut, never to open their doors again. British victims of the fallout of the 2007–8 crisis included the record-shop chain HMV,[18] the furniture company MFI, and – of course – our preferred Pic'n'Mix vendor, Woolworths.

Closures of this kind lead onto the second economic consequence of crises: unemployment. When businesses shut, people lose their jobs. Scaled up across a whole economy, lay-offs of this kind can be disastrous. During the Great Depression, one in every four American workers found themselves unemployed – and if you're out of a job during a recession, it's usually hard to find a new one. Some groups of people are more affected than others. Typically, younger and lower-skilled workers are the hardest hit. Workers aged 18 to 30 experienced higher unemployment and larger falls in real wages than any other group during the 2007–8 financial crisis.[19]

Once the economy recovers most people will find new jobs, sometimes in different industries. For example, after the financial crisis of 2007–8 some out-of-work bankers retrained to become science teachers.[20] But as we saw in Chapter Three, if people are unemployed for a long period of time they may permanently lose skills, rendering them less employable in the long run – meaning that the fallout from economic crises can affect people for decades. If a downturn lasts long enough, lower-skilled workers may stop looking for work all together – they realise that their chances of getting a job are slim and potential wages are low.

Which leads us onto the third economic effect of crises: greater inequality. In recessions, income inequality grows and poverty becomes more widespread. Between 2009 and 2010, during the fallout of the crash, the 1 per cent with the most wealth saw their incomes rise by nearly 12 per cent, while the remaining 99 per cent of the population saw their incomes stay roughly the same.[21] In other words, only the top earners saw the benefits of recovery, rather than the whole population. The same pattern followed the financial crash of 1929 and the resulting Great Depression. Between 1920 and 1928, the income share of the top 5 per cent rose from little more than a quarter to more than a third.

Why do recessions have this effect? There are several reasons. One might be that those who were already worse off are likely to have less education, and so have fewer job opportunities if they find themselves unemployed. Another might be that those with less income have fewer savings to lean back on if they do lose their jobs – making their journey to financial recovery more difficult.

Such dynamics play out not just between income groups, but between generations. In the wake of the 2008–9 financial crisis, the percentage of British children earning more than or equal to their parents declined. This strengthened the relationship between the earnings of parents and the earnings of children. Suddenly, inheritance became a more important factor in increasing your wealth. In the long run, recessions tend to undermine future generations' social mobility, which can have long-term consequences on the growth of an economy.

These economic problems only offer a glimpse of the full impact of recessions, however. Recessions affect every aspect of society – our lifestyles, our mood, our relationships. Consider the effect that the health of the economy has on the health of people. Most obviously, economic turbulence affects mental health. In the aftermath of the 2007–8 global financial crisis, as unemployment increased, suicide amongst men in the UK increased by more than 15 per cent.[22] Recessions affect people's physical health too. Today we have clear evidence that heart attacks and strokes increase during downturns.

Such health effects are borne not just by adults but also their children. Young people who grow up during economic instability are surrounded by stress and insecurity, which means they are at greater risk of developing mental-health issues. During the last recession, children's need for mental-health services increased by a half.[23] The depressing effects of depressions (and recessions) might explain the link between economic downturns and divorces. Divorce rates tend to increase after recessions as couples find it difficult to cope with financial strains – between 2003 and 2009 there was a general downward trend in the number of divorces, but in 2010 they rose by 5 per cent.[24] (On the flipside, after your divorce you're more likely to be asked out on a date. Research shows that people seek out others for first dates when the economy is in trouble – it seems economic turbulence makes people lonely.)[25]

All this hints that the myriad social and economic effects of recessions go far beyond simple metrics like unemployment, or growth, or wages. They affect every facet of our lives – even sometimes in positive ways. Take air pollution.

The collapse in Chinese manufacturing during the Covid-19 pandemic in early 2020 led to a sharp fall in air pollution, which will have some effect in reducing deaths in cities. In fact, some recessions have been shown to increase life expectancy. During the Great Depression, mortality rates in the US fell amongst areas of high unemployment – perhaps because people spent less on cigarettes, or got into fewer fatal traffic accidents on the suddenly deserted roads as fewer people were travelling to work.

If an economy can get through a recession, it sometimes tends to end up healthier, too. Economic crises usually ultimately lead to better companies that are more profitable. It's what the Austrian economist Joseph Schumpeter called creative destruction. Bad businesses go bust; so-so businesses have to step up their act to survive; and good businesses tend to be OK. This usually means that resources that would have gone to bad businesses are freed up to serve good businesses, or to set up new ones. A helpful example of creative destruction came in early 2000, when the Nasdaq stock exchange crashed after years of rising share prices in online companies. Businesses that had based their growth on excessive hype closed down. At the same time, the crash accelerated the rise of the less hype-prone and more genuinely viable online businesses, like eBay – ultimately changing the practices of billions of consumers.

Where does all this leave us in answering the Queen's question? Well, it hints that to see an economic crisis coming you need to keep an eye on a few things. First, any signs of disruption in the global economy – whether that's a speculative bubble, a rapidly spreading pandemic, or a build-up of an unsustainable imbalance, such as people owing too much debt. Second, any decreases in consumer or business confidence, which have the potential to spread out across the whole economic system.

One of the roles of economists is to draw on all of this information and use it – sometimes unsuccessfully – to make predictions. If we were at the LSE at the time of the Queen's fateful visit, we might have told her that determining what will happen to the economy is much like predicting the weather. Both economists and meteorologists are bad at predicting at exactly what time there might be a downpour or an economic crash but they're both better at predicting the changing of the seasons, or general trends in the economy.

Meteorologists know it's likely to be warmer in August than it is in December in the northern hemisphere. If you live in the UK, you know to put away your thick woollen coat once it hits March (or, realistically, May). You know you'll be using your sunglasses less at the end of the year than in the middle. Similarly, economists know where the economy is in terms of a boom or a bust, otherwise known as a business cycle, and can predict whether the economy is more or less likely to be growing or shrinking. But just as there are some rare days on which you need your sunglasses in mid-December or an umbrella in August (again, not so rare if you live in Britain), there may be some times in the business cycle when the economic weather isn't quite what you'd expect. Similarly, economists might know that the economy is about to shrink but not be able to predict exactly when, or what exactly might trigger it.

So what tools do economists use to make their predictions – and even to spot those emerging crises? They build models. Just like the weather, the economy is complicated – too complicated for economists to fully understand what is happening (without help). It is a complex system made up of millions of people, businesses and governments that are interacting constantly. So to help better understand the economy, economists – just like meteorologists – use models to simplify the world. As we saw in Chapter Two, models are always a little off the mark – but they can also be useful. They help economists understand the impact of policies or the way in which different bits of the economy interact.

Most models – whether meteorological or economic – are built using two components. First, data, and in many cases, a lot of it. In the Bank of England we use more than 100 data sets, containing more than 100 million separate bits of data. Some of the most important data points we plug into our models are those that might indicate a burgeoning crisis – such as an increase in risky borrowing (as we saw in the lead-up the Great Depression and 2007–8 financial crisis), or a fall in house prices.

Increasingly, some economists are turning to more unorthodox data trends to identify trouble on the horizon. There are many subtle and peculiar signs that the economy might be about to enter a downturn. For example, a sharp decline in the usage of cardboard usually means a crisis is looming. As most of the world's non-durable goods are shipped in cardboard boxes, when sales of cardboard increase it means companies are producing more – and so employing more people. When demand for cardboard starts to taper off, economic confidence could be about to implode. A similar pattern can be seen in big-ticket purchases like camper vans. Declines in RV sales in 1989, 2000 and 2006 all came shortly before subsequent recessions.

In fact, one of the most accurate short-term predictors of a downturn is the number of articles in the *New York Times* and the *Washington Post* in which the word 'recession' appears – otherwise known as the R-index, created by the *Economist*. The higher the number, the more likely it is that a recession is on its way. It's a simple methodology, yet it has turned out to be surprisingly accurate, and it correctly predicted recessions in 1981 and 2001.[26] This perhaps reflects the self-fulfilling nature of crises; they tend to happen when more and more people start to worry about the economy, and so talk and write about it.

Second, assumptions. Economists (and meteorologists) make assumptions or judgements about the way the world works and they use that to determine what might happen next. In forecasting the weather, meteorologists make assumptions about how different weather systems interact with each other at different times in the year. They can do this because they see this type of weather pattern over and over again. Likewise, assumptions are also made in economic modelling. They might assume that only one part of the economy changes at a time. For example, economic models might predict a fall in the price of electric cars would lead to an increase in people buying these cars, but they might ignore the fact that wages have fallen or interest rates on loans to buy cars have increased, and so people are buying fewer cars in general.

One of the most consistent (and controversial) assumptions used in many economic models is that people are rational: the notion that most people, businesses and governments in an economy will act in a way that benefits themselves – as if they're the utility-maximisation machines we met in Chapter One. This leads economists to assume that, for example, during a downturn people will save more as they are uncertain about whether they will keep their jobs.

In many cases, these assumptions don't undermine the accuracy of the models. Until, that is, they do. Today, there is a booming sub-field in economics pointing out the whole host of ways in which people act irrationally – and so demonstrating that many traditional economic models are flawed. It is insights of this kind that underpin the discipline of 'behavioural economics' – so-called because it studies people's actual economic behaviour, which can be based on emotions, rather than the way that traditional economic models say they should behave. Such irrationality is everywhere. It's what leads us to have another drink in the pub even when we are disastrously behind our publisher's deadlines, and what tempts you to order a takeaway when you know you have a fully stocked fridge in the kitchen.

This irrationality means that, all too often, economists' models are off the mark. For example, during the South Sea Bubble, many economic models (if they existed at the time) would have assumed that people wouldn't continue to invest in its stocks once there clearly wasn't a reason for them to keep increasing in price. Or, in the 1990s, that people wouldn't have queued for hours to buy soft toys for an investment. People did. And most of them lost money.

As a result, the models often fail us. Think again of the weather forecaster comparison. In 1987, the BBC weatherman Michael Fish famously laughed off a viewer's suggestion that a hurricane was on the way. That night would bring the most destructive storm to hit the UK since 1703, hitting the nation with winds of up to 115mph, leaving hundreds of thousands of homes without power and killing eighteen people. Like weather forecasters, when economists get it wrong, they can get it very wrong. In 2007, the Bank of England had predicted 1 to 4.5 per cent growth over 2008; while noting 'turmoil in international financial markets', they failed to predict a global economic crisis was on the way.[27] This was economists' 'Michael Fish moment', as its former Chief Economist Andy Haldane called it. Except, in fact, economists have a much worse record than Michael Fish. Economists have failed to predict 148 of the past 153 recessions around the world since the 1990s.[28]

With all this in mind, you might ask why economists still depend on models to predict economic trends. The answer is: they remain the best method we have. Remember that no model is right, but some are useful. And so a flawed model, many economists would argue, is better than no model at all.

On 22 July 2009, a group of economists wrote to the Queen to offer a more considered answer to her question about the financial crisis.[29] The result of a forum at the British Academy of 17 June, the letter explained that some economists did foresee the crisis. The issue was, they didn't know what exactly would trigger it, when it would happen or how bad it would be. They were like those meteorologists being able to forecast rain but struggling to predict how much or when it would start.

Truth be told, many policymakers had written about the dangers of risky activities in financial markets – lots of them thought that banks lending mortgages to people who seemed unlikely to be able to pay them back was clearly a bad move. But most didn't make the link between a fall in house prices, problems in banks and wider issues across the economy – they didn't imagine that this quantity of unpaid loans in the banking sector could bring the entire global economy to its knees.

The letter also pointed out that in the build-up to the crisis, economic models had proven good at predicting small and near-term risks. The issue was that they weren't equipped for saying what they meant for other parts of the economy – or predicting the full extent of what would happen when things went wrong. These economists and their models didn't connect the dots.

A thoughtful answer, but one with only so much utility – particularly if Her Majesty was interested not just in responding to the last crisis but preventing the next one. Although connecting the dots improves economists' ability to spot crises, every crisis is different, and so it's unlikely that future crises will be identical to past crises. At heart, given the complexities of the economy and the people in the economy, it is difficult to predict when crises will occur and what will cause them. The economy does not always behave in the way economists think it will, because people are not rational.

So perhaps the shortest answer to the Queen's question is the best one. Predicting crises is hard, because the economy – and people – are complicated.

All this means that the role of economists isn't just to predict and prevent crises. In a complex world, it would be foolhardy to conclude that all crises even can be prevented. It falls to economists not just to prevent crises, but to react to them.

For the economy is something we can influence. There are many levers that governments and central banks can pull to manage it – whether that's to prevent a crisis, respond to one, or just keep things ticking over. And it's the role of policymakers in managing the economy that is the focus of our final question.

Chapter Ten
Can't we just print more money?

*On what on earth 'quantitative easing' is, why bridges
to nowhere might not always be a bad idea, and how
Lord of the Rings isn't the only New Zealand export to
go global.*

In the Spanish TV show *Money Heist*, a group of ingenious
bank robbers take it upon themselves to break into the
Royal Mint in Madrid. Their goal is to print money: over
2 billion euros. Their argument, passionately advocated
by their leader 'El Profesor', is that this isn't stealing from
anyone. It is new money, not money taken from someone
else's bank account – and so the heist is morally justifiable.

The show's drama rests on the audacity of such a
heist. Except, in truth, this isn't a million miles from what
the world's central bankers have been doing, legally, for
the last decade. Although they haven't literally turned

on the printing presses, and certainly not at gun point, in recent years central banks around the world have been creating money on a scale that would make even our Hispanic bank robbers blush. Since the global financial crisis of 2007–8, at the time of writing the Bank of England has created almost £1 trillion of new money and used it to buy things in the economy. That is almost £15,000 for each and every person in the UK. And we're not the only ones. The US Federal Reserve has created over $7 trillion, and the ECB has created a similar amount of euros, seemingly out of thin air.[1]

To understand why central banks have undertaken such an astronomical expansion of the money supply, this chapter will explore the economic levers that central banks can use to guide the economy. We'll explore how these levers affect you and the world around you, and ultimately what restrains the hand of central bankers as they hover above the money-printing button. And we'll delve into the other ways that governments can influence the economy, using taxation and spending to try to keep it running as smoothly as possible. It's a lesson in economic policymaking that will take us on a journey around the world and across time. That journey begins, of all places, in Japan in the 1990s.

The 1980s was a boom time for the Japanese economy. The country had become the darling of global capitalism, producing everything from high-tech gadgets like Walkmans to cars. Then, in the early 1990s, the bubble burst. Or, more accurately, two bubbles burst: a house price bubble and a stock market bubble. The consequence was a slowing economy, as people and companies started spending less.

As the economy slowed, inflation fell – because, as we saw in Chapter Six, lower demand means prices grow less quickly, or even reduce. The Bank of Japan needed a way to stimulate the economy and raise inflation. Their goal, similar to most central banks, was to keep prices stable – which in turn indicated a healthy amount of spending across the economy.

But how to achieve that goal? The Bank of Japan, like other central banks around the world, conducts its business by influencing the cost and availability of money in the economy – a process known as monetary policy – and in the 1990s, the weapon of choice for implementing monetary policy was interest rates.

Because central banks are the bank for other banks, they are in an important position. They can set the terms on which they will lend to those other banks when they need a little extra money. They can also set the interest rate that they will pay to other banks on any deposits held with the central bank – just like your high-street bank does for you. When central banks change these terms, it has a series of knock-on effects on the rest of the economy through a series of channels, known collectively as the monetary transmission mechanism. These channels are a little fiddly, but bear with us: they're important.

First, by changing the rate they charge and pay to other banks, central banks induce those banks to, in turn, change the rates that they charge borrowers and pay to their depositors. This operates in a variety of ways. Most straightforwardly, take a tracker mortgage – its interest rate changes in line with the interest rate set by the central bank. The central bank interest rate has less direct consequences, too. Banks compete against one another to offer the best rate and attract customers – when the central bank switches its interest rate, this makes it more or less expensive for banks to offer deposits and lend. This means they either need to pass on any changes in costs to their customers or lose out to competitors who will. Eventually, the central bank's rate feeds through to a whole range of interest rates in the economy, from credit cards to bank deposits, business loans to savings accounts.

This in turn affects people's economic behaviour. Interest rates influence whether you should spend now or save now and spend later. Say you had £100 now, but if you stored it away it would turn into £110 tomorrow. There's not much in it: you might choose to spend it now, or you might not. But what if someone told you if you didn't spend it today, you could have £200 tomorrow? Would that shift your decision? Although an extreme example, this case study sheds light on how interest works across an economy. Higher interest rates increase your incentive to save and decrease your incentive to spend or invest; so when interest rates go up, more people save, fewer people spend, fewer businesses invest – and the economy slows. On the other hand, lower interest rates decrease your incentive to save and increase your incentive to spend today, adding a boost to the economy. With characteristic creativity, economists have named this process the interest rate channel of the monetary transmission mechanism.

Second, interest rates are linked to the value of assets in the economy. These might be financial assets such as stocks, or physical assets such as houses. When interest rates go down, the prices of these assets tend to go up.

That means people holding assets are better off. And when people get richer, they tend to go out and spend some of their increased wealth. A prime example is people borrowing a bit more when the value of their house goes up, then spending it. In this way, lower interest rates lead to an increase in wealth and, in turn, an increase in spending – again, giving a boost to the economy. This is known as the wealth channel of the transmission mechanism.

Third, there are what economists call income effects. Importantly, these will affect you differently if you are a saver or a borrower. If you are a borrower, lower interest rates mean you have to spend less each month on your mortgage payments. This means you have more money in your pocket. And as we've seen, when you have more money you're likely to spend more – again boosting the economy. On the flipside, if you are a saver, lower interest rates now mean you are getting less each month on your savings. Your monthly income has actually gone down, and you are likely to respond by reining in your spending.

The truth is that most of us are both savers and borrowers – we have money in our bank account and a mortgage, for instance – so your personal income effect will depend on the balance of those factors.

The strength of income effects across an entire economy depends on the balance of savers and borrowers, and how much each group changes its spending in response to changes in income. If both savers and borrowers have the same sensitivity to changes in their income, then the equal but opposite income shifts of savers and borrowers would balance out – so there would be no change in spending overall. However, economic evidence suggests that borrowers are more likely to spend a larger part of their new-found income than savers are to rein in their spending, meaning the income effect from a reduction in interest rates tends to boost spending in the economy.

Fourth, there are a group of channels that work through the banking system itself. When interest rates are lower, banks can offer loans to people more cheaply – so the amount of lending in the economy tends to increase. For a start, there is more demand for loans, as people look to borrow to fund their spending and investment today. At the same time, banks are more willing to lend – not least because the cost of issuing and maintaining a loan is lower, and people have more valuable assets to offer as security, thanks to the wealth channel. As we saw in the previous chapter, this increase in lending boosts the money supply, and also boosts economic activity, by allowing people to spend and invest. All of this leads to increasing demand, and so an increase in inflation.

The final channel of transmission is particularly important for a small, internationally connected economy like the UK. This is the effect on the exchange rate. When central banks lower interest rates, this tends to lower the exchange rate – sterling falls in value when UK interest rates fall. If the interest rate in the UK goes down, but the interest rate in the US doesn't, then you are going to get a relatively better return if you switch your money out of pounds and into dollars. So money flows across borders and more people want to buy dollars and sell pounds. This shift in demand means that the price of switching from pounds to dollars – the exchange rate – changes, making it more expensive to buy dollars with pounds. This in turn pushes up the prices of imports, which – as we saw in Chapter Six – pushes up inflation.

Still with us? Good. But there's one final complication. All of these mechanisms take time to work their way through the economy. Monetary policymakers cannot just click their fingers and suddenly inflation springs up or slows down. It is a bit like a sharpshooter aiming at a moving target: they have to aim ahead of where the target is when they pull the trigger, because they know it will have moved by the time the bullet reaches it. Likewise, when interest rates move it takes a while for the results to come into effect. This means that policymakers are constantly trying to set policy for where they think the economy will be, not where it actually is.

These lags are not particularly well understood and can be different at different times and in different conditions. In most instances, though, the effects of monetary policy take between six months and two years to be seen in the price inflation all around us. One important consequence of this is that if inflation is high today because of something that has already happened, but it is not expected to last, there is little that central banks can do about it. If they were to increase interest rates in response to inflation today, by the time that rate rise had an effect, the temporary inflation would have gone – they would merely be slowing the economy at a time they didn't need to.

The economists at the Bank of Japan understood all these processes well. As inflation fell, they cut interest rates. From 1991 to 1995 they cut the interest rate they charged to banks that were borrowing from them from 8 per cent to 0.5 per cent. This was a drastic change and took interest rates to a lower level than they had been at any time in Japan's history to that point. Yet it wasn't enough. Prices continued to slow, and even to fall. Here, the Bank of Japan encountered a new problem. Their weapon of choice was out of ammo. They had hit the much-feared 'lower bound': the point at which interest rates could fall no further.

Prior to this point, the lower bound on interest rates had been a largely theoretical concept – discussed in dark rooms by men in tweed jackets and written about in journals that almost nobody read. The theory went that interest rates could not go below zero, because if they did, everyone would just hold their money in cash. Cash essentially pays an interest rate of zero.[2] When other interest rates in the economy are high, this seems like a poor offering, so people tend to hold relatively small amounts of cash. But as interest rates get lower, cash seems relatively more attractive. When interest rates get to zero, the theory says, cash and other forms of money are basically equivalent. If the interest rate fell below zero the incentive would flip – everyone would want to hold cash. You would be crazy to pay someone to borrow money when you could earn more just by taking it all out of the bank.

'What nonsense,' some of you may already be saying. 'Of course interest rates can go below zero. It has happened – in the Euro Area, in Switzerland, even on some of the UK government's debt.' In practice, the lower bound is not zero, it is slightly below. Does this mean the theory is wrong? Not really, just that the real world is a little bit messier than the theory. In the real world there are costs to holding cash. Can you imagine if you were a big company holding your annual revenues in £50 notes? You would need a warehouse and some security guards to look after it. It might also be that huge piles of cash don't meet your needs – they might be a lot harder to transfer across the world to people you need to pay. Or it may be that cash just doesn't do what you need it to. Pension funds are responsible for paying out to their customers over long periods of time, and the amount they pay varies as interest rates move. That means cash, whose value doesn't shift in the same way in response to interest rates, is less useful to them than, say, a chunk of government debt that varies more closely with the value of their obligations to pensioners.

All of these costs and imperfections mean that you might be willing to hold your money as bank deposits or in other assets even if they paid negative interest rates. The cost is worth it. The lower bound is not zero, then – it could, in theory, be at least a little bit negative. But there certainly is a lower limit. How far into the minus numbers interest rates can go is an ongoing discussion among economists, and likely varies across countries and at different times depending on how resilient a country's banking system is, as well as the relative costs of storing cash (how much those warehouses and security guards would cost you, and so on). In some economies it may be lower than -1 per cent.

In 1990s Japan, though, there was considerable uncertainty around negative rates and how practical they were, and also what the side-effects might be for the rest of the financial system. There was a concern that even if rates could go negative, they might damage the already fragile banking sector by squeezing their profits and hurt savers – of which there are a lot in Japan. So the Bank of Japan took an alternative route. Decades before a Spanish crime series made the idea alluringly glamorous, they began printing money. This printing of money aimed to increase the quantity of money in the system and ease the economic slowdown, and so it became known as quantitative easing – though sometimes it goes instead by 'asset purchase programmes', or simply 'QE'.

How does QE work in practice? It's not quite as simple as running off more banknotes. Instead, the central bank buys something from people or companies in the economy. This is usually an asset without much risk to it, like a government bond – basically a chunk of government debt, like an IOU from the state. Central bankers prefer to use assets of this kind because they don't like the idea of taking on much risk. We're a cautious bunch. Then when the time comes for the central bank to pay for what they've bought, rather than using money they already have, the central bank simply adds some money to the account that the seller's bank holds with them. Some zeros are put onto the balance and that commercial bank in turns adds that money to the seller's account with them.

It's an ingenious mechanism, if we central bankers might say so ourselves. The seller ends up with fewer bonds but holds more money. The commercial bank now has a new deposit with the central bank, but has a matching deposit that they owe to their customer. The central bank also now has a bond that is matched with a deposit to the commercial bank. So overall, more money has been created from scratch – without the need for a printer.

By the mid-2000s, the Bank of Japan was doing this on what felt like a huge scale. It was seen as unorthodox, a move that was very specifically bound up with the peculiarities of the Japanese economy. As such, while it was interesting to discuss, QE wasn't expected to be necessary for anyone else. Some economists even estimated that the world would only be at the lower bound – and in need of their back-up policy option, QE – one year out of every fifty.[3]

This is not, in fact, what happened. Fast-forward to 2008, and the situation in the global economy might have felt disconcertingly familiar to anyone who had studied Japan. A collapse in the housing market was transmitted to the rest of the economy via a financial sector that was more fragile than people had expected. Central banks around the world cut their interest rates and found themselves at the lower bound. Now it wasn't just the Bank of Japan that had run out of space to use their primary weapon – interest rates – to counter the economic shock.

One man who had studied the Japanese economy and QE programmes was Ben Bernanke. He had been an academic economist for much of the 1980s and 1990s, researching, among other things, the causes of the Great Depression in the US, and the improvements that could be made to economic models if they more realistically included the financial system. He also watched what was going on in Japan with interest and wrote a number of papers and speeches on it. But in 2007, when the first signs of an impending global crisis began to show, Bernanke was relatively early on in a new job: Chairman of the US central bank, the Federal Reserve.

When the crisis broke, drawing on his knowledge of the past, Bernanke advocated that the Federal Reserve largely follow the prescription of Japan, although with some upgrades in the detail.[4] In 2008 the Fed began buying financial assets – first mortgages and then government bonds – from the economy using newly created money. Other central banks around the world did the same. QE had gone global.

Although an advocate of QE, Bernanke recognised that there were still some outstanding issues around the method. He famously once told perhaps the closest thing that economists have to a joke, saying that 'the problem with QE is that it works well in practice, but not in theory'.[5] This wasn't a criticism of QE per se. It was more a recognition that, while economists have found that QE does prove effective at lowering interest rates and boosting inflation, we don't yet have a full understanding of how.

Compare this to the world of medicine, an arguably more rigorous scientific counterpart to economics. Anyone who has ever had surgery will likely have been put under general anaesthetic. A doctor will have sent you into a deep sleep, rendering you oblivious of the fact that a limb is being sawn off or your internal organs tickled. And yet, until very recently, scientists didn't really have much of a clue about how general anaesthetic worked. They knew it did, they could see it in the data and test and calibrate with pretty good accuracy, but they weren't sure of the mechanism.[6] Did that mean that when you were in a medical emergency you refused to use anaesthetic? We would guess not.

Economists find themselves in a similar position with QE. Obviously we have theories on how increasing the money supply would drive inflation. We've encountered them already in this book. However, the problem the Bank of Japan faced was a different one: that mainstream theory at the time suggested that, when interest rates were so low they couldn't go any further, people just wouldn't want any more money. They had all the money they needed: if you gave them more they would just squirrel it away and not spend it. And, because interest rates were zero, if you swapped newly printed money for, say, some government debt – which would also pay no interest – then they wouldn't see any difference between the two pieces of paper. They wouldn't change their behaviour in any way. This situation is known as a liquidity trap.

So why did economists turn to QE, if the mainstream theory of the day suggested it wouldn't do much at exactly the moment it was needed? The answer is: a combination of revisiting the main theory in a new light, and revisiting some theories that had fallen out of fashion in the years before the 2007–8 crisis.

In the standard economic model that had prevailed through the 1990s and 2000s – the so-called New Keynesian model – if QE worked, it was only because it helped to shape people's expectations about what would happen to the economy and to interest rates. Expectations are a powerful force: what you imagine will happen in the future can shape your decisions today. In particular, when a bank is thinking about what interest rate to set on a thirty-year mortgage, it takes into consideration what the central bank's interest rates will be like today, tomorrow, and every day for the next three decades. As such, it will set the interest rate it charges on its expectation of all of those short-term rates. And so expectations of short-term rates in the future build up to determine the interest rates on longer-term borrowing today. It's a little like the way expectations of inflation can affect the actual rate of inflation, as we explored in Chapter Six.

In the New Keynesian model, such expectations about interest rates are practically all that matter. In a series of highly influential papers, the Columbia University economist Michael Woodford had argued that the best way to keep the long-term interest rate low was simply by making a credible promise: that central banks would keep rates low for longer than people expected. This promise became known as 'forward guidance'. In the original incarnation of Woodford's theory, you didn't need QE to keep the economy ticking over – just a strong promise that interest rates would remain lower for longer.

In later papers, Woodford would come round to QE, at least a little bit. But only because he thought it sent a signal to the economy about what would happen to interest rates: QE signals to the economy that a central bank is taking on lots of debt, whose value is connected to interest rates. This sets up central banks to make big losses if they put up interest rates sooner than they had promised. Policymakers are not big fans of losing money and so QE acts as another way by which central banks could declare to the wider world that they would keep interest rates low. In the New Keynesians' analysis, signals about the future rate of interest were always key.

All this made perfect sense, until it collided with economic reality. After the turmoil of the late 2000s, economists came to realise that the New Keynesians' analysis rested on some strong assumptions about the efficiency and rationality of financial markets. They turned to a separate body of theory, largely neglected in the run up to the financial crisis, that offers a different explanation of why QE works.

A key part of Woodford's arguments was that money and bonds were pretty much the same thing, especially when neither paid interest. Money and bonds were just different types of financial asset, each largely fulfilling the same role. But what if bonds were, in fact, substantively different to money? In the mid-twentieth century, economist James Tobin and others had thought about a world in which people viewed assets as 'imperfect substitutes' – crucially, they wanted to hold them for reasons other than just the interest rate they paid. The upshot of Tobin's framework was that swapping one thing for another – in the case of QE, money for bonds – has enormous implications.

If you don't see a bond as the same as money, then someone swapping one for the other is going to leave you with more money than you want, and fewer bonds. There is a high chance that you are then going to pass that extra money on to someone else. As you try to pass on some of that new money, the prices of things get forced upwards, and our central bankers are back on track towards their inflation target.

After the financial crisis of 2007–8 hit, it would eventually lead to an epiphany – that in many respects Tobin was right, and that the New Keynesian model didn't work quite as perfectly as might have been assumed. Today, most economists think that QE operates through a combination of forces. Signalling, yes, but also by rebalancing the amount of bonds and money that people hold – known as 'portfolio rebalancing'. And it works. It leads to interest rates that are lower and that stimulate spending and investment – and it also nudges up the rate of inflation. Since 2008, central banks have been able to use QE to help shepherd the global economy through the economic troubles that followed the crash.

All this might make you think that the answer to our question – Can't we just print more money? – is very simple: Yes, we can. After all, QE clearly has a beneficial impact on the economy when it's in trouble.

But there's a limit. You can't just keep on ramping up the money supply indefinitely. To understand why, we need to go back in time and around the world – this time to New Zealand in the 1980s.

Long before Peter Jackson had helped turn the country into a global tourist hotspot by filming *The Lord of the Rings* there, New Zealand was a small, sparsely populated and arguably often-under-rated country at the very bottom of the globe. Forgotten, that was, until 1989. New Zealand was the epicentre of a shockwave that had nothing to do with the various earthquakes that hit the country that year. It sent aftershocks around the global economy, although the vast majority of the population may not have known it even happened. The event? The establishment of a central bank independent of the government, given an explicit target – set down in law – to keep inflation at a certain level. While it may not have seemed that significant at the time, within twenty years this model had proven so successful that it had been emulated by almost every advanced economy in the world.

In the 1960s and 1970s, New Zealand, like much of the world, had been plagued with high inflation. In New Zealand's case this meant double-digit rates of inflation for most of the 1970s. A large part of the problem was that interest rates were not set independently by the central bank – they were set by politicians. This meant that while the politicians said they would keep inflation low, when the time came to act and put up interest rates to achieve that goal, they would hesitate or change their minds. They knew it would be unpopular. After all, higher interest rates would slow the economy, which is rarely a vote winner. People cottoned on. They expected inflation to be higher than the politicians said. As we saw in Chapter Six, these expectations meant that inflation did ultimately turn out to be higher.

Some of the finest economists of the time wrestled with this problem and termed it inflation bias. A solution, proposed by among others the American economist-cum-chess grandmaster Ken Rogoff, was to take the decision-making away from politicians. Instead, it should be in the hands of central bankers – who would be told to aim for an explicit target for the level of inflation.

This idea gained traction through the 1980s, but it wasn't until New Zealand took the plunge that it was properly tested in practice. The results were impressive and almost immediate. Within a few years, inflation had dropped to the target level, and become considerably more stable and predictable.

Where New Zealand led, others followed. In the UK, within a week of being elected in 1997, the incoming Labour government gave the Bank of England operational independence – with a remit to keep inflation low and stable.[7] To achieve this goal, they created a new committee of decision-makers, the Monetary Policy Committee, and gave them complete control over how they hit the inflation target, and how they set interest rates to achieve that.

The Bank was still accountable to Parliament if it didn't achieve this objective and inflation went too high or too low. But politicians could no longer interfere in the process of getting there. This was a far cry from what had come before. Former Bank of England Chief Economist Andy Haldane once said that, before the Bank of England's independence, the best predictor of interest rate movements was 'was whether Mrs Thatcher (the then Prime Minister) had recently suffered a bad by-election result'.[8]

The success of independent central banks targeting inflation directly has been palpable. Having averaged more than 10 per cent in the 1970s and 1980s, global inflation fell to 5 per cent in the 1990s, 3 per cent in the 2000s and just 2 per cent in the 2010s.[9]

What does this mean for our money-printing question? With great power comes great responsibility – and the flipside of independence for central banks is that they are tasked with protecting the value of our money, and keeping inflation low and stable. This means that while they get to set the terms of interest rates – or, in the case of QE, get to have their finger on the button of the printing press – they cannot do so without limit.

When inflation is looking like it will be lower than it should be, it makes sense to increase the amount of money: that means more QE. That will lead to more inflation and get the economy back to its target. But once that move begins to push inflation too high, printing more will become a problem and, as we learnt in Chapter Six, this has a cost to the public – reducing their spending power and, for many, increasing the cost of doing business.

All this means that central banks can print more money up to a point. But not endlessly – lest the economy falls into another age of uncomfortably high price increases, and we fail to hit our inflation target. Increases in money must be just right. These are the decisions that we at the Bank of England spend our days grappling with, and we do so without the direct input of the government.

But that doesn't mean that ministers have no role to play in guiding and stabilising the economy. We can start to make sense of how the government fits into economic management by returning, once again, to 1990s Japan.

The Japanese phrase *hakomono* most closely translates to English as 'white elephant'. It is a phrase that became increasingly common in the 1990s and early 2000s as the Japanese government spent huge amounts of money to try to stimulate the economy out of recession. Their efforts were focused on large infrastructure projects. Between 1991 and 2008, the Japanese government spent the equivalent of $6.3 trillion on construction-related public investments. They built dams, roads and perhaps most (in)famously, bridges. One such project, which cost over $250 million, was a bridge between one large island, Okinawa, and a smaller one, Kourijima – which had a population of fewer than 400 people. Another was the art gallery in Nagoya that cost so much there was nothing left over to buy art to fill it.

While the conventional wisdom is now that it is better to take monetary policy out of the hands of politicians, governments still have control over projects like these. They retain the power to tax and spend: fiscal policy. And large government-spending projects can have a beneficial impact on the economy – even if they are sometimes branded *hakomono* at the time.

In fact, the Kourijima bridge may even have found a supporter in one of the most important economists of the modern age. John Maynard Keynes once claimed that it was better for the government to pay people to bury money in a hole, dig it up and then pay them to fill the hole in again, than to leave people unemployed.

How can this be the case? To understand the answer, we first need to get to grips with why governments spend money in the first place. States spend for any number of reasons. They might want to subsidise a virtuous activity that is under-produced due to an externality, like subsidising further education. They might want to invest in a large-scale infrastructure project that benefits from economies of scale and so might not otherwise be built – like a road, or a tunnel under a sea. Or they might want to redistribute money from one part of the economy to another to address social inequalities.

But they may also spend to provide a boost to the economy when it needs it – a fiscal stimulus. When a government spends money, it buys things from other people in the economy, much the same as if any of us did so. The government could buy uniforms for police officers, medical equipment for nurses or new wheels for a bus. It might be concrete and steel for bridges and the wages of the workers who build them. This money increases economic output. It's the G in the GDP equation we saw in Chapter Four. So when spending is slowing down, and growth or inflation is becoming sluggish, government spending can give the economy the support it needs.

This last statement is not without controversy. There is considerable uncertainty about the desirability and effects of using fiscal policy to actively stimulate the economy. Traditionally, fiscal policy has often been thought of as 'too slow and too political'.[10] It can be too slow due to practical constraints. For example, delivering new major infrastructure projects takes time: you need to design and plan where and how a new school will be built long before boots can hit the ground.

From a political perspective, the use of fiscal policy could be subject to the same issue found in relation to monetary policy – with politicians incentivised to always spend more today, with the promise of paying for it in the future. Ultimately, this could jeopardise the long-run sustainability of public debt.

Even if these challenges can be overcome, how much government stimulus actually works is a topic of fierce debate. The row centres around a concept known as the fiscal multiplier. In one of his biggest contributions to economic thought, Keynes postulated that the effect of government spending on the economy could be significantly greater than just the money spent, especially when the economy is sluggish.

Think of those people digging a hole; their digging would count directly as economic activity, albeit not very productive activity. But they would not just keep the money to themselves. As they now had more money in their pockets, they would spend more – especially if they had been in desperate need of money for basics beforehand. Their spending is then increasing economic activity in other parts of the economy, pushing up demand for more people's goods and services. Say they bought an additional loaf of bread for their families. The baker is in turn likely to spend some of the money they receive – and so the cycle continues. At each stage, more economic activity happens, and this adds up to a greater boost to economic output than the initial spending by the government.

In this view of the world, the government spending has been multiplied up, hence the term 'multiplier'. Keynes' theory grew in prominence throughout the 1930s and 1940s and was a crucial influence on the New Deal initiative – President Franklin D. Roosevelt's response to the Great Depression, which involved massive increases in state expenditure. Advocates of Keynesian policies would say that the multiplier on government spending is usually greater than one, meaning you get out more than you put in. Every pound spent grows the economy by £1.50, say.

But critics would argue that this isn't always the case, and that you might even end up with a smaller boost in the economy than the money you put in was worth. They argue that spending a pound only leads to growth of 90p, or even less. There are a few reasons for this. The first might be down to the other policymaker in the game, monetary policy. If the government spends and boosts the economy, one of the results is likely to be inflation. What do central banks do when they think inflation is rising? They raise interest rates to cool the economy down again. These higher interest rates discourage people from spending and companies from investing – and so they offset some of the new spending that is being done by the government.

The second reason relates to where the money has actually come from. The government needs to get the money it is spending from somewhere, and that somewhere is ultimately from us, the taxpayers. As we'll see in a moment, taxes mean that we taxpayers have less to spend – courtesy of the tax man. The fall in our spending might even be greater than the new spending done by the government – dampening the fiscal multiplier.

This leads us onto the third reason: a concept called Ricardian Equivalence – named after the nineteenth-century economist David Ricardo, who we last met in Chapter Five. The theory goes that when the government spends more, people realise that they will eventually have to pick up the tab in higher taxes, so they rein in their own spending today to prepare for that eventuality – and completely offset the boost the government is trying to create.

All this remains controversial, particularly the notion of Ricardian Equivalence. Most economists now suggest that there are a number of reasons why Ricardo's theory doesn't hold in the real world. For a start, the people paying the taxes are not the same as those receiving the money from government spending. Add on to that the fact that few of us are thinking about government taxes in twenty years when making our spending decisions now, and also that people's behaviour can often be viewed as less than economically rational – a requirement for Ricardian Equivalence to hold – and you start to see how it can break down.

All these arguments and counter-arguments for the fiscal multiplier have made it one of the most controversial ideas in economics. If you want a fun game to play at a dinner party with a bunch of economists, ask them what the value of the fiscal multiplier is, then sit back and enjoy your dessert as they do battle.[11] Estimates vary from less than one to well over two – which would mean every pound spent gave you more than double that amount in economic benefit.

However, where most economists would agree is that the value of the multiplier depends on the exact nature of what the government is spending its money on, how it is paid for, and what else is going on at that moment. At a time when interest rates are very low and so is inflation – as was the case in Japan in the 1990s – the fiscal multiplier may be particularly high: monetary policymakers would actually be grateful for a little help lifting inflation, so they would not raise interest rates to offset the fiscal boost. Keynes himself suggested that fiscal spending would be particularly effective as a way of boosting the economy when spending was undesirably sluggish – the government would be taking the money that people were choosing not to spend and get it flowing in the economy. So those bridges to nowhere in liquidity-trapped Japan may have not been quite as silly as they sounded.

Of course, what the money is spent on also matters. In general, spending on a big infrastructure project that boosts growth for years to come is better than spending on day-to-day frivolities, or a bridge that very few people actually want. Or, for that matter, on people digging holes and filling them back in again.

Spending is not the only fiscal lever that governments can pull, however. The other is taxation. We've all paid taxes at some point or another: whether it is the value added tax (VAT) that we pay when we buy clothes, or the income tax that disappears from your pay cheque every month. Along with borrowing, taxes are one of the two main ways that money comes into the government's coffers. And it isn't new. Remember those ancient Mesopotamian tablets we talked about in Chapter Seven? They contained records of taxes paid. Perhaps Benjamin Franklin's famous edict that nothing is certain in life except death and taxes was more accurate than you might think.

As with spending, governments introduce taxes for a variety of reasons – from fixing externalities to raising money for big projects. And as with spending, they can redistribute between groups in society: some are 'progressive' – meaning they fall disproportionately on the rich – and others are 'regressive' – meaning they fall disproportionately on the poor. But taxes can also be used by governments to boost or slow the economy.

Taxes act in the opposite way to government spending in terms of the economy. While spending boosts demand and economic activity, taxes reduce it. Why? Because taxes are taking money out of people's pockets and pay cheques which they then cannot spend on other things. Meanwhile, cutting taxes puts money back into people's pockets and therefore acts as a boost to demand. In theory, this can have a similar multiplier effect to increased government spending – you're leaving more money out there to be spent. And, as with government spending multipliers, the debate rages between economists about exactly how large those multipliers are.

All this means that balancing spending and taxes is a key part of how governments can act to stabilise the economy. In some cases, they don't actually need to do very much. Government policy has been designed in a way that automatically provides a boost when things are slowing down and a brake when they are going too fast. When an economy is doing badly, the amount the government spends on things like welfare payments goes up. More people becoming unemployed automatically means more money spent on benefit payments. At the same time, people are earning less and spending less, so tax receipts from all areas go down automatically. This adds an almost inevitable boost to the economy, just when it needs it. Conversely, when the economy is booming, without doing a thing, the government will find itself spending less on welfare and benefit payments, because more people are in work, and it will find its tax income increasing as people earn and spend more.

This acts as a relative break on the fiscal boost provided to the economy. All of this can happen automatically, without a government minister having to change a single piece of legislation or make a single policy announcement. Such mechanisms are often called the economy's 'automatic stabilisers'.

This all raises a question: can the government indefinitely cut taxes and increase spending, forever boosting the economy? The answer, perhaps obviously, is no. Unlike central banks, governments cannot print their own money: that is the whole point of independent central banks. As such, whenever anyone asks the first great question of fiscal policy – How do we best stimulate the economy? – it leads inevitably to the second – How do we pay for it?

When the government's spending exceeds the amount it has coming in in taxes, then the gap must be filled by borrowing. Governments do this by offering bonds – those state-sanctioned IOUs we encountered earlier. They are usually bought by large financial institutions who need to tuck their money somewhere safe for a relatively long time: the pension fund looking after your money for retirement, or insurance companies offering life insurance policies that might pay out in many decades' time, for instance.

Were a government not to repay these debts, the consequences would be disastrous. It does happen. On 26 December 2001, the Argentinian government delivered an unwelcome late Christmas present. After more than three years of recession, the country's leaders realised the state would be unable to pay the debts it owed. Argentina defaulted on over $95 billion of obligations. Rather than pay back in full, the Argentinian government offered lenders just 30 cents for every dollar they had lent. At the time of writing, the court cases resulting from this default are ongoing.

This wasn't the first time Argentina had defaulted on its debt, and it wasn't the last. Argentina's history is sadly littered with defaults. Such unreliability means that those lending to Argentina want a lot more compensation to make the risk worth their while. And so the interest rate on Argentinian government bonds is closer to 50 per cent than the lower levels in other economies, many of which are near zero. That makes it harder for Argentina to borrow, and in turn fund those useful projects that are a major part of a state's economic arsenal.

Argentina is certainly not alone in having defaulted on its obligations. However, in general, most governments can be relied on to repay their debts. As such, they have some of the lowest borrowing costs in the economy. But how much debt it's acceptable for governments to have remains a hotly contested question. Economists remain divided over whether it's acceptable for governments to continually run a deficit. This is when taxes are less than spending, with the deficit being the gap between the two (the opposite, when taxes are more than spending, is known as a surplus).

A common analogy is that, like every good household, you must at some point tighten your belt and pay back the money you've borrowed. But the household comparison is less than perfect. First, governments don't die (even if specific administrations do). They can continue to pass forward borrowing over a much longer horizon than you or I, individuals who are ultimately constrained to eighty-odd years if we're lucky. What's more, say a government has decided to build a new motorway: it will cost £1 billion to build, but they think it will generate £2 billion for the economy in the long run. It borrows money to pay for it. When the time comes to pay off their loans, the government has a bigger economy to tax – and so the motorway has paid for itself. Even though the amount of debt has gone up, the amount of debt relative to the size of the economy has gone down.

At the same time, as economies tend to increase in size over time, the amount of debt relative to the economy will naturally fall – provided the new debt being taken on is less than the rate at which the economy grows. Imagine your economy is growing at 2 per cent per year, and you are charged 1 per cent interest. This means you can borrow up to 1 per cent of the size of your economy and still see the debt to GDP ratio fall. In fact, if trying to pay down your debts means that you have to tax so much or spend so little that it slows your growth, then the very act of trying to sort out your finances can become self-defeating. If you slow your economic growth to zero, your debt is going to become a much bigger problem.

This dynamic was seen clearly in the Greek economy at the turn of the 2010s. Many countries in the Eurozone found themselves struggling to pay off the interest on their debt – often because they had spent so much bailing out failing banks and supporting their economies through the previous financial crisis. The problem was particularly pronounced in Greece. But as the Greek government implemented austerity measures that cut back state spending and raised taxes – and so aimed to reduce the scale of their debt – the impact was to slow economic growth and reduce the tax base available to continue paying the debt. The then Managing Director of the International Monetary Fund, Christine Lagarde, would later concede that her institution had miscalculated the fiscal multiplier when advocating such policies. They had assumed it to be less than one, when in reality it was closer to 1.7 – and so the IMF pressured the Greek government to cut the state ill-advisedly.[12] Just as fiscal boosts could have oversized positive effects when a multiplier is greater than one, austerity policies can have a negative effect in the same situation.

Now, even the most strident Keynesian economists would accept that at some point, if your borrowing is so high that people question your ability to repay it then you can hit issues. Should you get a reputation like Argentina, then your cost of borrowing will increase – and taxpayers, now or in the future, will have to bear the brunt. And so high interest rates on government bonds can be a problem.

However, the debt level at which that problem kicks in in most rich economies has been shown to be pretty high. Often public discussion focuses on the point at which the debt owed reaches 100 per cent of the size of the economy. Yet a longer view shows that for the last 100 years, the UK government has had a ratio of debt to GDP of 100 per cent or more for almost half of the time – and has generally not had serious concerns around its ability to pay.

In one of the climactic scenes of *Money Heist*, El Profesor offers a rationale for the economic benefit of breaking into the Spanish Royal Mint. After being cornered by the dedicated police officer who has been pursuing him, he offers a crash course in economic history. 'In the year 2011, the European Central Bank made 171 billion euros out of nowhere,' he says. 'Just like we're doing. Only bigger.'

She looks suspicious. But El Profesor is unshaken. '"Liquidity injections", they called it,' he tells her. 'I'm making a liquidity injection but not for the banks. I'm doing it here, in the real economy.'

Does El Profesor have a point? In general, this book is not in favour of bank heists. However, he was right that printing money can work, through a range of channels, to support activity in the economy. In doing so, it can raise inflation when it looks like it might otherwise be too low. In fact, this is one of the ways – alongside governments using their powers of taxing and spending – central banks have kept the economy stable in recent years, especially when they have found their usual tools of the trade – like setting interest rates – have reached their limits.

But there's a limit. If central banks were to continue to print more and more without limit, the result would be too much inflation, with prices rising uncomfortably fast and eroding the value of the newly printed money at too fast a rate – potentially making people worse, not better off. This is why, unlike the daringly charming Spanish bank robbers in *Money Heist*, the Bank of England's money printing has been done in the pursuit of a very clear objective. It is aiming for an inflation target set for central banks by democratically elected law-makers – one that means money-printing is unlikely to spiral out of control in future.

Conclusion
You, the economist

It was a warm July evening in 2019, and Charlene Maines was standing in a small queue outside the doors of the Central Hall, a community centre in Southampton.[1] On your average weekday, the building's meeting rooms would be playing host to a Women's Institute meeting, a yoga group, or perhaps a touring comedian. But this Tuesday, the assembled cast included a group of central bankers. And Charlene was on the guest list, even if she wasn't quite sure why.

The Central Hall was hosting a Bank of England Citizens' Panel, one of a dozen such panels set up across different parts of the UK to allow members of the public to meet Bank of England policymakers and discuss their experiences of the economy. On that night in Southampton, unbeknown to the twenty-five or so participants, the line-up featured none other than the Bank's Governor at the time, Mark

Carney. Charlene, a thirty-seven-year-old charity worker and carer, had come along more out of curiosity than anything else, having spotted an advert for the panel in her workplace. But as the 6pm start time approached, she began to regret it. Having been born in Liverpool, around 200 miles away from the Bank's imposing doors, Charlene felt the country's economic policymakers existed in another world. She was nervous about what the evening might have in store.

The problem was the economists themselves. She thought they were 'stuck-up, posh and boring', she later said. At the event, she even put on a 'posh' voice to fit in. Her perception of economics as a discipline was no better. She considered it to be full of ideas that were too complicated to understand, with policymakers constantly using bewilderingly technical language and incomprehensible models. The confusing nature of economics had even deterred Charlene from voting in the Brexit referendum in 2016: she felt she didn't have enough understanding to make an informed decision.

But a few minutes into the panel event, Charlene's impression of economics had started to shift. She realised that putting on a fake accent was unnecessary – and that she had more in common with the economists than she had thought. It turned out that both Charlene and the former Governor supported the same football team, Everton. Economics, meanwhile, proved to be much simpler than she had been led to believe. For all its complex words, the discipline merely described things she had come across in her day-to-day life. Truth be told, she had understood economics her entire life – just in different terms to those that economists used. She was using economics every time she went to the shop, or paid her rent or applied for a new job.

Upon leaving the event, Charlene sought out ways to increase her understanding of the economy. She started to read up on economics on the internet and signed up for adult evening classes. It was life-changing. A couple of years on, she runs a charity designed to help get people out of long-term unemployment – which she was inspired to do having experienced a long period out of work herself. She credits her increased understanding of the economy with helping her find a career and then helping others do the same. Her new-found love of economics induced her to take a greater interest in politics, too. She now chairs her local branch of a political party and is running for councillor in her constituency. Charlene often speaks to her peers about how economic policies affect the things that matter to her, her family and the local community.

Charlene's experience is far from unusual. She was not alone in disliking economists. In one survey of the most trusted professions in Britain, economists ranked second from bottom – with only politicians lower.[2] Nor was she alone in believing that economics, done right, had the potential to improve her quality of life. In 2019, nearly 50 per cent of people reported wanting to increase their understanding of economics.[3] The issue was that all too many of them didn't know where to start.

Having got this far, we hope that you've been on a journey similar to Charlene's. You might agree with her that economics isn't as inaccessible as it seems. And while it's easy to couch economics in the language of academic theory, it can also explain the experiences that make up our daily lives.

We began our journey with the most basic principles underpinning economics: supply and demand. Economists use an admittedly crude shorthand to make sense of human behaviour: assuming that the choices we make are governed, directly or indirectly, by our desire to maximise our 'utility'. Charlene might point out that if this insight sounds abstract, it is actually anything but. Every time you make a choice about whether to splash out on a holiday (or not), you are implicitly making a utility trade-off: between the money it will cost you and the happiness it will bring you. Markets are little more than the cumulative effect of these millions of trade-offs, rippling out across a society.

As we learnt in Chapter Two, these markets are brilliant at getting us the things we need. Until they aren't. Because markets can also be dysfunctional – leading to good outcomes for some individuals, but much worse ones for society. This operates at a global level – think climate change – but also in your day-to-day life. The next time you're at a Happy Hour, ponder the implications of market failure. If you buy a pitcher of a drink – say a jug of Pimm's – you're likely to end up with less drink than you would just buying your own glass. As a public good, the pitcher is meant to be shared between you and all your friends. But for the same reason, everyone is more inclined to drink faster than they would otherwise. The Tragedy of the Commons in your Pimm's round means that, almost inevitably, some people at the table lose out.

From market failures, we turned to labour markets. Why do some people get paid more than others? And why is it so hard to build an economy in which everybody has a job? The answers lie in the interplay of supply and demand, which determine how much work there is for people to do. But labour markets are inefficient. However hard we try, the 'frictions' inherent in applying for a job will always mean there is some unemployment. This principle is not only relevant to jobseekers. You can apply the same insight to dating. Even if the world was filled with a perfect number of compatible singletons looking for love, there would still always be single people. Why? Because, as with jobs, matching up romantic partners is hard. You might go to bars five nights a week but still never meet the perfect person – they could be going to the bar up the road. And while dating apps help us quickly identify who is single – improving what an economist would call 'matching efficiency' – they can still never fully eradicate frictions in the 'market' for romance.

In Chapter Four, we moved on to growth. We are almost unimaginably richer than our ancestors 500 years ago. That's because of the growing size of the economy – the increasing amount of stuff that is shared between the people who use it. If this sounds like a detached concept, again it is anything but. Indeed, you can grow your own output in much the same way that you would grow an economy: through the interplay of land, labour, capital and technology. Say you're thinking of buying a new laptop. By upgrading to one with a longer battery life, you are making yourself more productive. You'll spend less time running for a charger. Perhaps you would be able to take your laptop to work in the garden, where you feel more relaxed and achieve more. By combining your labour with better capital, you're able to get more done – growing your personal economic product.

Chapter Five explored why all your clothes are made abroad. It's because of comparative advantage: the notion that, when we all focus on what we're good at, it can be better for everyone. This principle will affect you every time you go to a dinner party. Say you and your friend are both asked to contribute a different dessert. You've decided that between you you'll bring a tiramisu and crème brûlée. Your friend is a good cook – she even goes to night classes. She has an 'absolute advantage' in dessert making, and you would be happy for her to make two dishes – except you have to contribute something, and she doesn't have time to make both. So how do you choose what to cook? You remember she specialised in making French desserts in those classes – so would make a better crème brûlée than tiramisu. That's her comparative advantage. As a result, you choose to make the tiramisu. Everybody wins.

Perhaps when you went to buy the cream and coffee for your dessert, you noticed they were pricier than you'd hoped, certainly more so than when you last made this recipe. The reason is inflation: the tendency of goods and services to increase in price. Inflation is entwined with all of our daily economic decisions. For example, during the beginning of 2020, the run on toilet paper caused inflationary pressure: there was a surge in demand as people stockpiled toilet roll, in fear of being caught short during the pandemic. It was an extreme example of the demand-pull inflation we met in Chapter Six.

In practice, however, none of these economic examples make any sense without money. It's money that allows us to buy things, sell things, exchange things. But what actually is money? As we saw in Chapter Seven, it is nothing more than a system of trust. It is a little like when you lend your friend some money when they forget their bank card at the shop. You wouldn't typically make a friend sign something to promise that they will pay you back (or, at least, your friend might look at you oddly if you did). You simply trust they will. This, at heart, is all that money is. Just like a £20 note, the trust that your friend will pay you back is another type of money. It could be as valid as a £20 note, as long as you trust your friend as much as you trust your central bank, and other people do too.

Of course, people don't always trust their banks, and while Chapter Eight hopefully convinced you to store your money in a bank account rather than under your mattress, people sometimes ignore this advice. The result can be bank runs. When banks get into trouble, we central bankers are sometimes on hand to help them out. But not always: we don't want other bankers to think we'll always be there to help, however much they screw up. In this, we central bankers are making the kind of trade-off that millions of people make every day. Think back to your time at school. As a teenager you might have usually got the bus to school in the morning, but when your parents were home, you may have been more inclined to hit the snooze button repeatedly. Why? Because there was no incentive to get out of bed early if you knew your parents would drive you to school if you missed the bus. This is moral hazard applied to your morning routine.

The trouble is that schoolchildren, just like the rest of us, are not always good at assessing the knock-on impact of their actions – whether to parents or to the taxpayer. Chapter Nine taught you why most economists didn't see the 2007–8 financial crisis coming. To be fair to economists, it's hard to predict when crises will happen. People don't always behave in the way we think they will: they're not rational. The conflict between our tendency to assume that people are rational and their actual behaviour defines all our lives. Bear this in mind the next time you see a queue outside a new restaurant. Ask yourself: are people queuing because the food is actually good, or just because the act of queuing sends a signal that it is, and so it's worth waiting in a queue for hours? Some of the people in the queue may just be queuing because others are – it's herd behaviour. You might be better off going to the restaurant next door where you can get a table straight away – and where the food might be better (and cheaper).

Finally, there's the role of us economists not just in describing the economy but also trying to manage it. Governments and central banks can pull a variety of levers to keep the economy running smoothly: from increasing public spending to stimulating a sluggish economy, tweaking interest rates to, yes, sometimes creating more money. It can be difficult to see how these decisions impact you. But they do. Every time the Bank of England's Monetary Policy Committee meets to make a decision on the interest rate, it can have a bearing on the exchange rate the next time you go on holiday, or the price of your mortgage repayments, or whether you should put a bit more money in your savings account or spend it now.

So Charlene was right – economics matters. And it matters whether you're used to the formal language of economics or not. In fact, you've probably been thinking like an economist for your whole life. Just maybe you didn't know it.

But economics won't merely help you understand the world; it can help you change it. Every time you make a choice to buy or not buy something, you're sending a signal to the person selling it – as well as the business making it – about whether you are or are not happy with what they are offering. By buying a cup of coffee, a Freddo or a Beanie Baby, you are influencing how the markets for them work. There are more direct ways that economics can empower you to change the world, too. Economics can help you bargain more convincingly for a pay rise at work, respond more effectively to climate change, even participate more constructively in democracy.

The more you know about economics, the better you understand the society you inhabit. We set out to write this book because all too many people don't understand economics – as Charlene discovered at the panel event in Southampton. Studies have found that the British public understands very little about this discipline. People say they feel that economics is 'inaccessible', 'confusing', 'complicated', 'difficult to understand', and the list goes on.[4] One particularly shocking poll from May 2017 – just before a UK general election – found that over half of the UK public didn't feel confident that they understood the economic impact of the policies they were voting on.[5]

This lack of economic understanding is a problem. It's not just that you might cook a dessert in which you don't have a comparative advantage, or join a queue for a restaurant that turns out to be disappointing. You might also vote for economic policies that don't work for you or store your savings in the wrong place. For the same reason, when you understand economics you can get more out of your weekly shop, your job, your politicians and even your life. Improving your economic literacy can make you wealthier, healthier and perhaps even happier.

Our hope, then, is that this book has not just taught you a little about economics, but that it has inspired you to find out more about it. Having read this book you should understand the basic building blocks of economics: supply, demand, inflation, recessions and so on. But there is a whole world of economics we didn't cover. We haven't touched on game theory, which can help explain everything from how to win a game of chess to how politicians can avoid a nuclear war. Or development economics, which explores how to improve the economic health of low- and middle-income countries. All of these subsets of economics build on the principles we've introduced here – utility maximisation, the law of demand and the power and problems of markets, and so on – but take them in new and exciting directions.

All these sub-disciplines hint that economics is no longer merely found in dusty textbooks in libraries. It is increasingly embedded in the world around us, and drawing from an ever-wider array of parallel disciplines. Even in the days since we were learning economics at university, its culture has transformed. Nowadays you can learn about economics by listening to podcasts, browsing social media or plucking one of the ever-growing number of pop-econ books from the shelves – books just like this one.

Along the way, many of the most well-established economics arguments are being challenged from all sides. Economics needs these challenges. For that to happen, economics needs economists – economists who aren't just experts with a penchant for maths and lots of letters after their names. It needs amateur economists who take on the irrationality that sometimes takes hold of the economics profession (we're not immune to the odd bout of animal spirits ourselves). And it needs economists who break the mould, bring fresh ideas and have different experiences.

So close this book and empower yourself to become a better economist. You are the economy and so you have the power to shape it and be shaped by it. Along the way, you might just help create a better society for everyone.

Appendix
Economics in 51 Even Simpler Questions

Acknowledgements

This book wouldn't have happened without the input, support and guidance of a whole army of people. It really has been a team effort.

First and foremost, we must thank Andrew Hebden for coordinating things and keeping the show on the road. Without him there wouldn't have been a book for anyone to read. We are also incredibly grateful to his colleagues in the Bank of England's Communications directorate James Bell, Sebastian Walsh and Mike Peacock, who between them got the Bank of England into the business of writing books and gave us the opportunity to be a part of it. And, of course, to the Bank's Governor, Andrew Bailey, for supporting the project and contributing the foreword. We would also like to give a special mention to Charlene Maines, a member of the Bank's Citizens' Panel, for talking to us so openly about how joining the panel has changed her view about economists and economics.

We owe a special thanks to our wonderful editor, Rowan Borchers, who patiently taught us how to write a book. And to Joanna Taylor and the rest of the team at Penguin Random House, whose expertise and dedication have been invaluable throughout. Thanks also to the Bank's agent, Adam Gauntlett at PFD, for connecting us with the Penguin team in the first place.

At the Bank we are fortunate enough to work with some of the brightest economic minds around, and even more fortunate that so many of them are such generous people that they have given up their time and expertise to help shape this book. We drew on the specialist knowledge of a number of colleagues to sketch out the most important content. They also pointed us in the direction of many of the most interesting examples and cultural references that have brought the material to life. So, if you enjoyed any of our case studies, and perhaps even learned something, then you should join us in thanking: Will Abel, Lena Anayi, Nicholas Butt, Shiv Chowla, Rupert de Vincent-Humphreys, Aydan Dogan, Rebecca Freeman, Tom Key, Simon Kirby, Lewis Kirkham, Simon Lloyd, Andre Moreira, Doug Rendle, Harry Rigg, Austen Saunders, Simon Scorer, Brad Speigner, Ryland Thomas, Boromeus Wanengkirtyo, and Carleton Webb.

We would also like to thank the army of fact-checkers that diligently corroborated (or corrected) our informed assertions and 'rough' numbers. Without them, you would have read many more square brackets. For this we thank: Leanne Aubard, Martina Babetto, Randip Bains, James Barker, Giulio Bianchi, Mark Billenness, Frances Cassidy, Joseph Chilvers, James Clay, Zara Coe, Keiran Corbett, Jem Davis, Daniela Donohoe, Ben Dovey, Nicole Edmondson, Ihsaan Faisal, Caroline Fosdike, Maren Froemel, Frances Furness, Joe Ganley, Ben Harris, Himali Hettihewa, Sudhanshu Jain, Louise Johnston, Volkan Karaboyun, Benjamin

King, Martina Knopova, Thomais Kotta Kyriakou, Tom Lappage, Jayson Lee, Owen Lock, Zachary Morris-Dyer, Debra O'Connor, Bartholomew Oram, Ameera Osmani, Manisha Patel, Anjum Pervez, Gerry Pimm, Milo Plunkett, Kyle Richards, Pierre Sanoner, Edo Schets, Harry Sleep, Katie Taylor, Robert Taylor, Anna To, Thomas Viegas, Dylan Viswambaran, Kai Walker, Donna Western, Sofia Whiteside, and Christopher Wilder.

Throughout, we benefited hugely from conversations with colleagues and friends whose expert eyes and instincts let us know when we were drifting into the dull and academic. You brought us back to the real world, so thank you: Adam Barlow, David Baumslag, Michael Bennett, Sarah Breeden, Richard Button, Matthieu Chavaz, Charlie Dyos-Hunter, Andrew Gimber, Rashmi Harimohan, Rich Harrison, Maggie Illingworth, Ben King, Lizzie Levett, James Montille de Bizouard, Isabel Sanchez, Rhiannon Sowerbutts, and Mo Wazzi.

And lastly, we would like to thank you, for taking the time to read this book. We hope you found it interesting, and maybe even fun.

Notes

Introduction

1 'Public houses and bars, licensed clubs, licensed restaurants, unlicensed restaurants and cafes, and takeaway and food stands, London, 2001 to 2020', www.ons.gov.uk

2 'Sea level rise in London, UK', www.open.edu, 4 February 2020

3 Smith described himself as a moral philosopher, a subject he taught at the University of Glasgow. In fact, the term economist wasn't really a thing back then.

4 'The art and science of economics at Cambridge', www.economist.com, 24 December 2016

5 'Change is needed in the next generation of economists', www.ft.com, 4 October 2021

6 This is actually when the term economics came into common use, as a shorthand for economic science.

7 'A First Look at the Kalman Filter', julia.quantecon.org

8 For more on this, see Kate Raworth's fantastic (and tasty) work on 'doughnut economics'. Kate Raworth, *Doughnut Economics* (Random House Business, 2017)

9 'ING-Economics Network Survey of the Public's Understanding of Economics', www.economicsnetwork.ac.uk, May 2017

10 'Public Understanding of Economics and Economic Statistics', www.escoe.ac.uk, 25 November 2020

11 www.annamarialusardi.com, 30 October 2020

12 Rethinking Economics Survey, yougov.co.uk, 2016

13 Andy Haldane's speech on 'Everyday Economics', www.bankofengland.co.uk, 27 November 2017

14 This subsequently expanded out to the UK more widely as various unifications occurred.

15 'The history and the founding of the Bank of England', www.bankofengland.co.uk

16 Montagu Norman, quoted in Andy Haldane's speech 'Thirty years of hurt, never stopped me dreaming', www.bankofengland.co.uk, 30 June 2021

17 You can become part of this by visiting www.bankofengland. co.uk/get-involved

18 We can't believe we're that old, either.

Chapter One: Where does my breakfast come from?

1 Yes, we know. That one winds us up too.

2 'Spending decisions that show our limitations', www.ft.com, 6 April 2018

3 'Happy hour specials boost alcohol sales', www.bevindustry. com, 17 October 2018

4 Hopefully more if you are outside of London.

5 Strictly the elasticity refers to percentage changes in price, which complicates our carrier bag example, as the price change from zero is an infinitely large percentage. However, the point about a small change in price leading to a large change in behaviour holds.

6 'Drug goes from $13.50 a tablet to $750, overnight', *New York Times*, 20 September 2015

7 'The price elasticity of demand for cigarettes in the UK, 2001–2011', academic.oup.com, 1 October 2013

8 'Smoking and Health: Report of the Advisory Committee to the Surgeon General of the Public Health Service', www.cdc. gov, 11 January 1964

9 'Statistics on Smoking – England 2019', digital.nhs.uk, 2 July 2019

10 'Comparison of trends of self-reported consumption and sales in England, 2011 to 2018', jamanetwork.com, 28 August 2019

11 Although cigarettes have also become more expensive.

12 'Meat consumption per capita', links between meat consumption and climate change, Guardian Datablog, 2016

13 'How China could change the world by taking meat off the menu', Time.com, 22 January 2021

14 'Does everyone really order the second-cheapest wine?', Alex Mayyasi, www.atlasobscura.com, 3 May 2018

15 Alfred Marshall, *Principles of Economics* (Macmillan, 1890)

16 'Giffen Behavior and Subsistence Consumption', www.aeaweb.org, 4 September 2008

17 Milton Friedman, 'A Friedman doctrine – the social responsibility of business is to increase its profits', *New York Times*, 13 September 1970

18 'All eyes on shale as $50 oil makes U.S. wells profitable again', www.bloomberg.com, 28 January 2021

19 'Euro 2020 final tickets offered for £70,000 per pair for England's clash with Italy', www.thesun.co.uk, 11 July 2021

20 The Nobel Prize-winning economist Gary Becker once showed that the decision to get married can be characterised as a market, in which people aim to maximise their future output and take advantage of specialisation of labour. The function of love in that setting is to reduce the transaction and monitoring cost of production, leading to a more productive outcome. Fine, but try putting that in a Valentine's Day card.

21 Adam Smith, *The Wealth of Nations* (W. Strahan and T. Cadell, London, 1776)

Chapter Two: Can economics solve climate change?

1 'The Tragedy of the Commons', Garrett Hardin, *Science*, Vol. 162, 13 December 1968

2 George Box, *Empirical Model Building and Response Surfaces* (Wiley-Blackwell, 1986)

3 Smith, *The Wealth of Nations*

4 'Vaccine monopolies make cost of vaccinating the world against COVID at least 5 times more expensive than it could be', www.oxfam.org, 29 July 2021

5 'Most popular social networks worldwide as of July 2021, ranked by number of active users', www.statista.com, 16 November 2021

6 Policies on tuition fees have differed across the various home nations of the UK and also in relation to the country of origin of students. For example, at the time of writing students who live in Scotland can get free university tuition if they stay in Scotland to study.

7 'What's a degree got to do with it? The civic engagement of associate's and bachelor's degree holders', Mallory Angeli Newell, *Journal of Higher Education Outreach and Engagement*, Vol. 18, No. 2, June 2014; and 'The relationship between graduates and economic growth across countries', Department for Business, Innovation & Skills, Research Paper No. 110, August 2013

8 'UK dependency on fossil fuels 1970–2020', www.statista.com, 8 September 2021

9 'Carbon footprint of electricity generation', Postnote update number 383, Houses of Parliament, June 2011

10 We'll come to a challenge to this view in a minute.

11 As with quotas, there is a difficulty in putting an accurate number on this in practice.

12 'How do emissions trading systems work?', www.lse.ac.uk, 11 June 2018

13 'The Market for Lemons', George Akerlof, *Quarterly Journal of Economics*, August 1970

14 'Amazon deletes 2,000 reviews after evidence of profits for posts', www.ft.com, 4 September 2020

15 Not unlike economics, at times.

Chapter Three: How do I get a pay rise?

1 'The impact of the Mariel Boatlift on the Miami Labor Market', *Industrial and Labor Relations Review*, Vol. 43, No. 2, www.jstor.org, January 1990

2 'Women's employment', ourworldindata.org, March 2018

3 'Vacancies by industry', www.ons.gov.uk, 16 November 2021

4 'The Relation between unemployment and the rate of change of Money Wage Rates in the United Kingdom, 1861–1957', A. W. Phillips, www.jstor.org, November 1958

5   Sorry, Jack.
6   'The degrees that make you rich ... and the ones that don't',
    Jack Britton, Institute for Fiscal Studies, www.ifs.org.uk,
    17 November 2017
7   'The Career Effects of Graduating in a Recession', www.nber.
    org, 11 November 2006

Chapter Four: Why am I richer than my great-great-grandma?

1   'Car ownership in Great Britain', David Leibling, RAC
    Foundation, Figure 2, p. 4, www.racfoundation.org, October
    2008; '1970 vs 2010: 40 years when we got older, richer
    and fatter', Michael McCarthy, *The Independent*, www.
    independent.co.uk, 23 September 2015
2   For what economists actually mean when they say 'in
    today's money' see Chapter Six, Office for National Statistics,
    'Average household income, UK: financial year 2020', Figure 2,
    www.ons.gov.uk
3   'Poverty, wealth and place in Britain, 1968 to 2005', Table 8,
    p. 16, Joseph Rowntree Foundation, www.jrf.org.uk
4   'A millennium of macroeconomic data', www.bankofengland.
    co.uk
5   'Life expectancy at birth in the UK', data.worldbank.org
6   'Remarks at the University of Kansas', Robert F. Kennedy,
    www.jfklibrary.org, 18 March 1968
7   'Changes to National Accounts: Inclusion of Illegal Drugs and
    Prostitution in the UK National Accounts', www.ft.com, 29 May 2014
8   'The value of adult and childcare, household housing services,
    nutrition, clothing and laundry, transport and volunteering',
    www.ons.gov.uk, 2 October 2018
9   This example draws on Mariana Mazzucato, *The Value of
    Everything* (Allen Lane, 2018)
10 'Growth is good for the poor', David Dollar and Aart Kraay,
    Journal of Economic Growth, Vol. 7, No. 3, www.jstor.org,
    September 2002
11 'GDP per capita', 'Life expectancy at birth', 'Mortality rate,
    infant', data.worldbank.org

12 'The world economy over the last two millennia', ourworldindata.org

13 'Population total, United States and China', data.worldbank.org

14 'Macroeconomic Effects of Japan's Demographics', www.imf. org, 28 November 2018

15 'The Effect of Population Aging on Economic Growth, the Labor Force and Productivity', www.nber.org, July 2016

16 'U.S. Census Bureau, Population Estimates and Projections, 2020', www.census.gov

17 'Labour Force by sex and age', stats.oecd.org; 'World Development Indicators', data.worldbank.org

18 'Labour Force by sex and age', stats.oecd.org

19 'Women at work, the key to global growth', www.spglobal.com

20 Ha-Joon Chang, 23 Things They Don't Tell You About Capitalism (Penguin, 2011)

21 'The happiness–income paradox revisited', Richard A. Easterlin, Laura Angelescu McVey, Malgorzata Switek, Onnicha Sawangfa, and Jacqueline Smith Zweig, www.pnas.org, 2010

22 'High income improves evaluation of life but not emotional well-being', www.princeton.edu, August 2010

23 'Easter Island's Collapse: A Tale of Population Race', sites. uclouvain.be

24 'Changes in the global value of ecosystem services', www.sciencedirect.com, May 2014

25 'Natural Capital and Environmental Net Gain', www.nic.org.uk, February 2021

26 'NGFS climate scenarios for central banks and supervisors', www.ngfs.net, August 2020

27 'Full cost of California's wildfires to the US revealed', www.ucl. ac.uk, 7 December 2020

Chapter Five: Why are so many of my clothes made in Asia?

1 The bookcase is so popular around the world that Bloomberg has created a Billy Bookcase Index comparing the price of the same shelf in different countries. It's a way of measuring Purchasing Power Parity or PPP, which measures how much stuff you can buy with the same amount of money in different countries.

2 'What are the triathlon "world records" for each distance?', *Triathlon Magazine*, 22 November 2021

3 There is no 40-kilometre cycling race, but the current record for distance covered in one hour stands at 55.1km, implying a time of 43:56 minutes for 40km. Taylor Dutch, 'Another world record for Joshua Cheptegei, this time in the 10,000 meters', *Runner's World*, 7 October 2020; 'Men Freestyle World Records', fina.org ; 'Cycling's World Hour Record', Bikeraceinfo.com

4 Adam Smith, *The Wealth of Nations*, 1776

5 'Results: Tokyo 2020 Olympic Games', triathlon.org, 26 July 2021

6 'The dark future for the world's greatest violin-makers', www.bbc.com, 8 July 2020

7 'The Silk Roads', www.nationalgeographic.org

8 John Maynard Keynes, *The Economic Consequences of the Peace*, 1919

9 'Trade and Globalization', ourworldindata.org, October 2018

10 'Average annual income of employees working for urban non-private units in China in 2020', National Bureau of Statistics of China, www.statista.com; 'National Occupational Employment and Wage Estimates United States', www.bls.gov, May 2019

11 'World Trade Statistical Review 2021', p.11, World Trade Organization, www.wto.org

12 'Supplier List', www.apple.com, 2021

13 'Globalization in transition: The future of trade and value chains', www.mckinsey.com, 16 January 2019

14 'The Multifibre Agreement', www.fibre2fashion.com; 'Statistics on Textiles and Clothing', Eurostat, 2019; Irene Brambilla, Amit Khandelwal and Peter Schott, 'China's Experience under the Multi-Fibre Arrangement (MFA) and the Agreement on Textiles and Clothing (ATC)', National Bureau of Economic Research, 2010.

15 'Bra Wars and the EU's China syndrome', www.politico.eu, 31 August 2005

16 'In focus – Trade protectionism and the global outlook', Monetary Policy Report, www.bankofengland.co.uk, November 2019

17 'Traffics, trains and trade; the role of institutions versus technology in the expansion of markets', www.nber.org

18 'RCEP: A new trade agreement that will shape global economics and politics', www.brookings.edu, 16 November 2020

19 'WTO's World Trade Statistic Review 2021', www.wto.org, Table A23

20 'Share of selected countries and regions in cross-border services exports in 2019', www.statista.com, April 2021

Chapter Six: Why aren't Freddos 10p any more?

1 With apologies to Kermit.

2 There is even a Freddo Index, at which you can see projections of the future price of Freddos: www.vouchercloud.com/resources/the-freddo-index

3 'How have prices changed over time', www.bankofengland.co.uk

4 'What's in every CPI basket around Europe?, www.vouchercloud.com

5 'Inflation basket of goods highlights seven decades of changing UL lifestyles', www.theguardian.com, 15 March 2015

6 'Making sense of consumers' inflation perceptions and expectations', www.ecb.europa.eu, 2021

7 'The Nokia 3310 just turned 20 years old – here's what made it special', www.techradar.com, 1 September 2020; 'Buy iPhone 12', apple.com

8 In an interesting example of shrinkflation, the current lottery now asks players to choose from 59, not 49 numbers, reducing the probability of winning.

9 If you turn to Chapter Eight, you'll learn the myriad reasons other than inflation that this is a bad idea.

10 Economist Phillip Cagan defined hyperinflation as when prices increased by 50 per cent in a month. That is equivalent to almost 13,000 per cent per year. For more cautious economists, the threshold is reached much lower, when rates are closer to 30 per cent per year.

11 'The magnitude of menu costs: Direct evidence from large US supermarket chains', www.jstor.org, August 1997

12 We can't believe she's charging her own grandchild interest either.

13 'Inflation, annual percentage of consumer prices, OECD total', stats.oecd.org

14 'The Counter-Revolution in Monetary Theory', Milton Friedman, 1970

15 John Maynard Keynes, *A Tract on Monetary Reform* (1923)

16 He actually said '*Cogito, ergo sum*', but even economics has learned to put away the Latin these days.

Chapter Seven: What actually *is* money?

1   'The gold standard: revisited', www.cbc.ca, 27 July 2011

2   And, strictly speaking, coins made by national mints, but these don't account for very much in the bigger scheme of things.

3   Hyman Minsky, *Stabilizing An Unstable Economy* (Yale University Press, 1986)

4   Some people believe that this is really a collective of people.

5   This was probably intended to verify the date of the block's creation, but was also quite pointed.

6   Possibly.

7   Although this is one of the many decisions that the Bank of England and other central banks are weighing up in thinking about future money. There is no fundamental reason it would have to pay interest.

Chapter Eight: Why shouldn't I hoard all my money under the mattress?

1   'Daughter throws away mattress stuffed with mother's $1 million life savings', www.theguardian.com, 10 June 2009

2   'Cash in the Time of Covid', www.bankofengland.co.uk, 24 November 2020

3   'Lindsey hoard: Coins stashed during Civil War declared treasure', www.bbc.co.uk, 14 August 2021

4   'Ten years after the financial crisis – two-thirds of British people don't trust banks', yougov.co.uk, 29 August 2018

5   'Household income, spending and wealth in Great Britain', www.ons.gov.uk, October 2020

6   'UK Payment Markets Summary', www.ukfinance.org.uk, June 2021

7   Benes and Kumhof, 'The Chicago Plan Revisited', www.imf.org, August 2012

8   More modest reforms that simply separated commercial and investment banking, lowering the risk taken with depositors' money, were implemented instead. The same Banking Act that established this separation in 1935 also set the terms on which the modern US central bank, the Federal Reserve System, is built.

9   'The Great Depression: An Overview', www.stlouisfed.org

10 Although others implemented the lender of last resort role much earlier: Alexander Hamilton (of musical fame) did so in the late 1700s when he was US Treasury Secretary.

11 'The Demise of Overend Gurney', www.bankofengland.co.uk, 2016

12 'Last Resort Lending, Market-making and Capital', www.bankofengland.co.uk, 28 May 2009

13 'The Effects of Automobile Safety Regulation', Sam Peltzman, *Journal of Political Economy*, 1975, Vol. 83, No. 4, pp. 677–725.

14 'Road traffic accidents before and after seatbelt legislation', www.ncbi.nlm.nih.gov

15 'Anything Worth Doing is Not Necessarily Worth Doing Well', link.springer.com, 31 January 2012

16 'Financial Stability Report', www.bankofengland.co.uk, December 2021

Chapter Nine: Why did no one see the crash coming?

1   'I did not stammer when the Queen asked me about the meltdown', Professor Luis Garicano, www.theguardian.com, 18 November 2008

2   'What Caused the Stock Market Crash of 1929-And What We Still Get Wrong About it', www.time.com, 24 October 1929

3   'Stock Market Crash of 1929', www.federalreservehistory.org

4   'Employment and unemployment in the 1930s', Robert A. Margo, *Journal of Economic Perspectives*, Vol. 7, No. 2, 1993, pp. 41–9.

5   'World Population by region', ourworldindata.org

6   'Understanding the depth of the 2020 global recession in 5
    charts', blogs.worldbank.org, 15 June 2020

7   'Breaking a fall', www.economist.com, 16 October 1997

8   'GDP growth', data.worldbank.org

9   *The South Sea Bubble; An Economic History of its Origins and
    Consequences* (Helen Paul, 2011)

10 'Review of Economic Bubbles', *International Journal of
    Information Management*, August 2016

11 Although Minsky's books were mainly found in the discount
    bin through the twentieth century, during the financial crisis of
    2007–8, many leading economists bought his book to help them
    make sense of what was happening. The Nobel Prize-winning
    economist Paul Krugman even named a high-profile talk about
    the financial crisis at the LSE 'The Night They Re-read Minsky'.

12 'Newton's financial misadventures in the South Sea Bubble',
    Andrew Odlyzko, royalsocietypublishing.org, 29 August 2018

13 'The Beanie Baby bubble of '99', thehustle.co, 19 May 2018

14 'US Stocks Fall 10% in Worst Day Since 1987 crash', www.
    ft.com, 12 March 2020

15 'GDP growth (annual %)', The World Bank, data.worldbank.org

16 'The financial crisis at 10: Will we ever recover?', www.frbsf.
    org, 13 August 2018; 'Measuring the macroeconomic costs
    and benefits of higher UK bank capital requirements', www.
    bankofengland.co.uk, 1 December 2015

17 'GDP growth (annual %) – Iceland', The World Bank, data.
    worldbank.org; www.sedlabanki.is

18 HMV was later saved by a restructuring company, Hilco, in
    2013 and continues to trade today.

19 'Unemployment by age and duration', www.ons.gov.uk; 'Real
    Wages and Living Standards in the UK', www.cep.lse.ac.uk, 2017

20 'Disillusioned bankers quit the City for the rewards of
    teaching science', www.theguardian.com, 23 November 2008

21 'Striking it richer: The evolution of top incomes in the US',
    eml.berkeley.edu, 2 March 2012

22 'Suicides in England and Wales', www.ons.gov.uk, 2021

23 'Child mental health in England before and during Covid-19',
    www.thelancet.com, 11 January 2021

24 'Divorces in England and Wales', www.ons.gov.uk, February 2014

25 'The Recession. Isn't it romantic?', www.nytimes.com,
    11 February 2009

26 'Don't mention that word', www.economist.com, 28 June 2001

27 'Inflation Report, February and November 2007', www.
    bankofengland.co.uk

28 'How well do economists forecast recessions?', www.elibrary.
    imf.org, 5 March 2018

29 'Letter to the Queen from the British Academy', www.
    ma.imperial.ac.uk, 22 July 2009

Chapter Ten: Can't we just print more money?

1   ' Credit and Liquidity Programs and the Balance Sheet', www.
    federalreserve.gov and www.ecb.europa.eu

2   The sometimes forgotten but influential German economist
    Silvio Gesell actually proposed a system for charging
    interest on paper money by charging a regular fee to stamp
    banknotes, or else they would expire and become worthless.
    This became known as a Gesell tax and has in various guises
    been discussed by economists including Irving Fisher and
    John Maynard Keynes.

3   European Central Bank, www.ecb.europa.eu, September 2003

4   Japan had largely spent its newly created money on buying
    things from the banks. However, some of these banks were
    in a bad way following the financial crash that had happened
    and so held on to the money rather than spending it. In the
    revamped QE set in motion by Bernanke and others, central
    banks bought directly from other people and companies,
    by-passing the banks and getting the money more directly
    into the economy.

5   'Bernanke cracks wise; The best QE joke ever!', www.cnbc.
    com, 16 January 2014

6   'Scientists unveil how general anesthesia works', www.
    sciencedaily.com, 27 April 2020

7   The original numerical target was 2.5 per cent on a measure
    of inflation known as RPI-X. This was later updated to be a
    target of 2 per cent consumer price inflation, or CPI.

8   'Thirty years of hurt, never stopped me dreaming – speech by Andy Haldane', www.bankofengland.co.uk, 30 June 2021
9   'Inflation: A tiger by the tail?', speech by Andy Haldane, www.bankofengland.co.uk, 26 February 2021
10 'Fiscal Policy Reconsidered', A. S. Blinder, brookings.edu, 20 May 2016
11 This may not actually be fun.
12 'IMF calls time on austerity – but can Greece survive?', www.bbc.co.uk, 11 October 2012

Conclusion

1   Author's interview with Charlene Maines, 20 October 2021
2   'Leave voters are less likely to trust any experts – even weather forecasters', yougov.co.uk, 17 February 2017
3   'ING-Economics Network Survey of Public Understanding of Economics 2019', www.economicsnetwork.ac.uk, November 2019
4   'Public Understanding of Economics and Economic Statistics', www.escoe.ac.uk, November 2020
5   'YouGov/Ecnmy Survey Results', yougov.co.uk, May 2017

Index